The Greatest Jesus Mystery of All Time

❦ THE LOCHLAINN SEABROOK COLLECTION ❧

CHILDREN
Honest Jeff and Dishonest Abe: A Southern Children's Guide to the Civil War
Saddle, Sword, and Gun: A Biography of Nathan Bedford Forrest For Teens

VICTORIAN CONFEDERATE LITERATURE
I, Confederate: Why Dixie Seceded and Fought in the Words of Southern Soldiers
Rise Up and Call Them Blessed: Victorian Tributes to the Confederate Soldier, 1861-1901
Support Your Local Confederate: Wit and Humor in the Southern Confederacy
The Bittersweet Bond: Race Relations in the Old South as Described by White and Black Southerners
The God of War: Nathan Bedford Forrest As He Was Seen By His Contemporaries
The Old Rebel: Robert E. Lee As He Was Seen By His Contemporaries
Victorian Confederate Poetry: The Southern Cause in Verse, 1861-1901
We Called Him Jeb: James Ewell Brown Stuart As He Was Seen By His Contemporaries

ABRAHAM LINCOLN
Abraham Lincoln: The Southern View - Demythologizing America's Sixteenth President
Lincolnology: The Real Abraham Lincoln Revealed in His Own Words - A Study of Lincoln's Suppressed, Misinterpreted, and Forgotten Writings and Speeches
Lincoln's War: The Real Cause, the Real Winner, the Real Loser
The Great Impersonator! 99 Reasons to Dislike Abraham Lincoln
The Unholy Crusade: Lincoln's Legacy of Destruction in the American South
The Unquotable Abraham Lincoln: The President's Quotes They Don't Want You To Know!

NATURAL HISTORY
North America's Amazing Mammals: An Encyclopedia for the Whole Family
The Concise Book of Owls: A Guide to Nature's Most Mysterious Birds
The Concise Book of Tigers: A Guide to Nature's Most Remarkable Cats

FAMILY HISTORIES
The Blakeneys: An Etymological, Ethnological, and Genealogical Study - Uncovering the Mysterious Origins of the Blakeney Family and Name
The Caudills: An Etymological, Ethnological, and Genealogical Study - Exploring the Name and National Origins of a European-American Family
The McGavocks of Carnton Plantation: A Southern History - Celebrating One of Dixie's Most Noble Confederate Families and Their Tennessee Home

MIND, BODY, SPIRIT
Autobiography of a Non-Yogi: A Scientist's Journey From Hinduism to Christianity (Dr. Amitava Dasgupta, with Lochlainn Seabrook)
Britannia Rules: Goddess-Worship in Ancient Anglo-Celtic Society—An Academic Look at the United Kingdom's Matricentric Spiritual Past
Carnton Plantation Ghost Stories: True Tales of the Unexplained from Tennessee's Most Haunted Civil War House!
Christ Is All and In All: Rediscovering Your Divine Nature and the Kingdom Within
Christmas Before Christianity: How the Birthday of the "Sun" Became the Birthday of the "Son"
Jesus and the Gospel of Q: Christ's Pre-Christian Teachings As Recorded in the New Testament
Jesus and the Law of Attraction: The Bible-Based Guide to Creating Perfect Health, Wealth, and Happiness Following Christ's Simple Formula
Mysterious Invaders: Twelve Famous 20th-Century Scientists Confront the UFO Phenomenon
Seabrook's Bible Dictionary of Traditional and Mystical Christian Doctrines
Sea Raven Press Blank Page Journal: For Reflections, Notes, and Sketches
Secrets of Celebrity Surnames: An Onomastic Dictionary of Famous People
The Bible and the Law of Attraction: 99 Teachings of Jesus, the Apostles, and the Prophets
The Book of Kelle: An Introduction to Goddess-Worship and the Great Celtic Mother-Goddess Kelle, Original Blessed Lady of Ireland
The Goddess Dictionary of Words and Phrases: Introducing a New Core Vocabulary for the Women's Spirituality Movement
The Greatest Jesus Mystery of All Time: Where Was Christ Between the Ages of 12 and 30?
The Martian Anomalies: A Photographic Search for Intelligent Life on Mars
UFOs and Aliens: The Complete Guidebook
Victorian Hernia Cures: Nonsurgical Self-Treatment of Inguinal Hernia
Vintage Southern Cookbook: 2,000 Delicious Dishes From Dixie
Your Soul Lives Forever: Documented Victorian Case Studies Proving Consciousness Survives Death

WOMEN
Aphrodite's Trade: The Hidden History of Prostitution Unveiled
Princess Diana: Modern Day Moon-Goddess - A Psychoanalytical and Mythological Look at Diana Spencer's Life, Marriage, and Death (with Dr. Jane Goldberg)
Women in Gray: A Tribute to the Ladies Who Supported the Southern Confederacy

REPRINTS
A Short History of the Confederate States of America (author Jefferson Davis; editor Lochlainn Seabrook)
Prison Life of Jefferson Davis (author John J. Craven; editor Lochlainn Seabrook)
Life of Beethoven (author Ludwig Nohl; editor Lochlainn Seabrook)
The New Revelation (author Arthur Conan Doyle; editor Lochlainn Seabrook)
The Rise and Fall of the Confederate Government (author Jefferson Davis; editor Lochlainn Seabrook)

Lochlainn Seabrook does not author books for fame and glory, but for the love of writing and sharing his knowledge.

∘⊛ SeaRavenPress.com ⊛∘

Warning: SEA RAVEN PRESS BOOKS WILL EXPAND YOUR ★ MIND!

The Greatest
Jesus
Mystery Of All Time

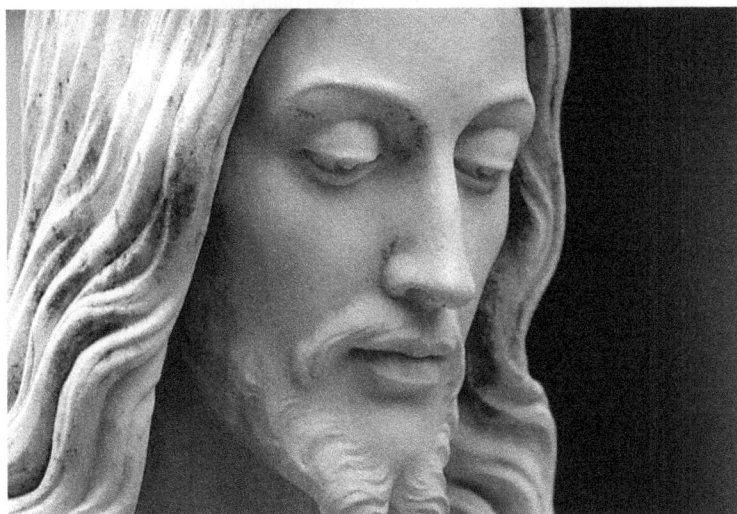

Where Was Christ Between the Ages of 12 and 30?

BY BIBLE-SCHOLAR, CHRISTIAN MYSTIC, & AWARD-WINNING HISTORIAN

Lochlainn Seabrook

JEFFERSON DAVIS HISTORICAL GOLD MEDAL WINNER

Diligently Researched and Generously Illustrated by the Author for the Elucidation of the Reader

2024

Sea Raven Press, Park County, Wyoming, USA

Published by
Sea Raven Press, Cassidy Ravensdale, President
Park County, Wyoming, USA
SeaRavenPress.com

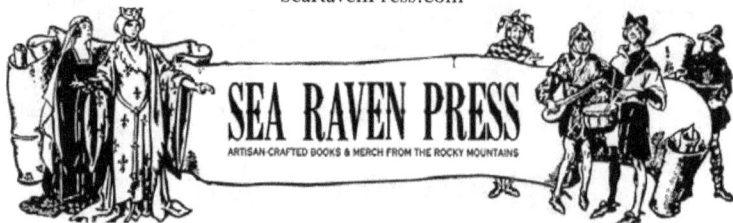

SEA RAVEN PRESS
ARTISAN-CRAFTED BOOKS & MERCH FROM THE ROCKY MOUNTAINS

PRINTING HISTORY
1st SRP paperback edition, 1st printing, March 2024 • ISBN: 978-1-955351-40-9
1st SRP hardcover edition, 1st printing, March 2024 • ISBN: 978-1-955351-41-6

ISBN: 978-1-955351-40-9 (paperback)
Library of Congress Control Number: 2024934261

The Greatest Jesus Mystery of All Time: Where Was Christ Between the Ages of 12 and 30? by Lochlainn Seabrook. Includes an introduction, illustrations, index, endnotes, and bibliography.

ARTWORK
Front and back cover design and art, book design, layout, font selection, and interior art by Lochlainn Seabrook
All images, image captions, graphic design, and graphic art copyright © Lochlainn Seabrook
All images selected, placed, manipulated, cleaned, colored, tinted, and/or created by Lochlainn Seabrook
Cover photo: "Jesus in Contemplation," Richard Paul Kane

The views documented in this book concerning Jesus and the "Lost Years" are those of the publisher.

WRITTEN, DESIGNED, PUBLISHED, PRINTED, & MANUFACTURED IN THE UNITED STATES OF AMERICA

REAL HISTORY MATTERS

Dedication

To my Lord

Epigraph

"And there are many other things which Jesus did, the which, if they should be written every one, I suppose that even the world itself could not contain the books that should be written."

Gospel of Saint John

Contents

SEA RAVEN PRESS

was founded for the express purpose of publishing and circulating such books as are calculated to store the mind with useful knowledge. We therefore publish only books of a high moral tone and tendency—such works as will be welcomed in every home and at every fireside as valuable family treasures.

L. SEABROOK

Introduction

CONTRARY TO WHAT THE PROVINCIAL mainstream Christian might think, my purpose in writing this book is not to undermine the Christian Church, Christian doctrine, or Christian tradition—as if that were even possible. And in my case, this would certainly not be necessary or desirable, for I respect and love the long-held customs and beliefs of my religion.

However, as both a Christian mystic and a writer-historian-researcher I take strong issue with myth being paraded as history, as well as history being paraded as myth, both practices which are regularly promoted and performed by the orthodox Church, and have been for the past 2,000 years.

In the following pages I present views and ideas that will be new to, and may be considered "radical," by some. In my opinion, however, they are neither. Facts are eternal verities, and are therefore never new or radical. They are simply realities that exist, whether we are aware of them or not. Either way, they are still facts.

I cannot prove that all of the concepts, stories, and views contained in this work are absolutely 100 percent authentic. I have not seen with my own eyes the ancient manuscripts I will be discussing. I have not personally interviewed those involved. I have not traveled to either the Middle East or the Far East to investigate every detail of the mysteries which I cover.

Instead, I present what I consider to be the best and the most probable factual evidence based on a myriad of supporting factors. When all are added together, a fundamentally different view of the life story of Jesus emerges; one far from that which we have been taught; but more importantly, one that does not harm Christianity, but instead, I believe, augments, forwards, and exalts it.

One should never be afraid to intellectually explore new ideas, new subjects, new theories. There is nothing to lose by this approach and everything to gain. The scientific method of inquiry, which I utilize across my studies and writings, requires that we accept whatever is uncovered, whatever it may turn out to be. Bending facts to fit our personal beliefs, preferred views, religious notions, or political ideologies is a terrible misuse of the awe-inspiring minds our Maker has so generously gifted us.

In the end my intent is never to convert, or even convince. I leave it to my readers to decide for themselves what is true and what is not true in my books. This one is no exception. Enjoy the journey.

Lochlainn Seabrook
Park County, Wyoming USA
March 2024
In Nobis Regnat Christus

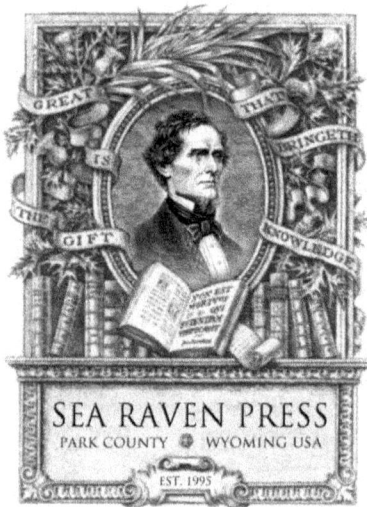

"Books invite all; they constrain none."
Hartley Burr Alexander (1873-1939)

Chapter One

A BIOGRAPHICAL PROBLEM

THE MYSTERY BEGINS

THERE ARE AT PRESENT SOME 2.6 billion Christians in the world, with at least 3.3 billion projected by the year 2050. This makes Jesus the most important person in human history to over a quarter of the world's population, a group in turn belonging to the largest organized religion in the world.

One would think that this level of importance would accord our Lord a complete, or, at the very least, a partial biography. But this is scarcely the case. There are *no* historically authenticated biographies of, or even mere references to, Jesus outside the Bible.[1] The few extrabiblical examples that have been discovered, such as several "comments" made by ancient Jewish historian Flavius Josephus (born around 37 AD, mere years after Jesus' death), seem to be forgeries. As in other cases of this kind, the references to Jesus found in Josephus' work (infamously known

Jesus of Nazareth.

as "The Testimonium Flavianum") do not match his writing style as a 1st-Century Jew, demonstrating that they were almost certainly composed and added later by unknown Christian propagandists.[2]

Discarding wholesale such specious "references" to Jesus, we are left then with only the New Testament.

THE GOSPEL "BIOGRAPHIES"

Sadly, here too things fall apart at the start, for we are met with barely a paragraph's worth of what could be deemed pertinent biographical material. Not even the date of our Lord's birth was recorded, leading to much confusion: The New Testament asserts that he was born, generally speaking, in the Spring,[3] while, under the Gregorian Calendar, modern Christians honor his birthday on December 25, a date borrowed from ancient Paganism which celebrated the return of the Sun-god/Son-god every year at the Winter Solstice. Some Greek Orthodox Christians mark Christ's birthday on January 7, also a date from the old Pagan Julian Calendar.[4]

A number of sources insist that Jesus, like Krishna, Apollo, and many other ancient savior-gods, was born in a cave;[5] others that He entered the world in a stable.[6] According to one Gospel (and one only), several astrologers ("magi" or magicians) visited Jesus at the time of His birth,[7] strongly linking the event with astrology—an occult science that is thoroughly repudiated by modern conventional Christians, who, due to a few specific Bible scriptures, link it with Satanism.[8] (This despite the fact that other biblical statements, including one from Jesus,[9] contradictorily promote astrology.)[10]

Mary and the baby Jesus.

To complicate matters, the world's only universally accepted "biographies" of Jesus, namely the four Gospels, sharply disagree with one another on key points: Matthew gives a different family genealogy for Jesus than Luke,[11] including different names for Jesus' paternal "grandfather," that is, the father of Joseph (Matthew calls him Jacob,[12] Luke names him Heli[13]); Matthew says that Jesus and his parents were from Bethlehem,[14] while Luke states that they were from Nazareth[15]—a town that many scholars believe did not exist in Jesus' time;[16] some biblical scriptures state quite overtly that Jesus was the "son of Joseph,"[17] while others assert that He was born supernaturally, the offspring of a virgin and an angel.[18]

Let us note here that if Matthew is historical, then Luke is unhistorical; if Luke is historical, then Matthew is unhistorical, calling the veracity of both into question. Either way, due to the many serious and incongruous issues between these two books alone—unless we imbue God with imperfect knowledge—it is for good reason that textual, form, source, and literary criticism has questioned the so-called "infallibility" of the Good Book.[19]

THE GOSPEL PROBLEM

This issue goes beyond Matthew and Luke, of course, encompassing all four Gospels. Dr. Albert Schweitzer wrote copiously on the many problems associated with this messy quadrangle of famous books, noting the "complete irreconcilability of the historical data" and "the want of any thread of connection in the material they offer us." The famed German theologian and philosopher made much of the discontinuity and paucity of authentic historical material they contained, stating:

Albert Schweitzer.

"While the Synoptics [the first three Gospels] are only collections of anecdotes (in the best, historical sense of the word), the Gospel of John—as stands on record in its closing words—only professes to give a selection of the events and discourses."[20]

Medieval theologian Martin Luther also despaired at the thought of making sense of the New Testament story of Jesus, writing:

"The Gospels follow no order in recording the acts and miracles of Jesus, and the matter is not, after all, of much importance. If a difficulty arises in regard to the Holy Scriptures and we cannot solve it, we must just let it alone."[21]

Is an accurate and genuine biblical biography of Jesus possible considering such facts? The field of biblical criticism argues no. Let us see for ourselves.

BIBLE TAMPERING

Examples of Bible meddling by nefarious unknown editors, along with their dire results, are unending and countless massive volumes have been written on the subject of the many omissions, contradictions, bowdlerizations, discrepancies, recensions, mistranslations, interpolations, Pagan borrowings, "corrections," expurgations, and redactions found in the so-called biblical "life of Jesus." One historian, Arthur Findlay, determined that the English revisers working on the King James Version of the New Testament alone made 36,191 "changes" during their translation from the original Greek text, a staggering average of 4.5 redactions in each of its 7,960 verses. [22]

And with each new translation, these "improvements" continue unabated into the present day. In my book *Seabrook's Bible Dictionary of Traditional and Mystical Christian Doctrines*, I write:

> "Bible scholars estimate that the Good Book has been so extensively revised and rewritten for doctrinal purposes that there is no longer a single sentence in, for instance, the New Testament in which the scriptural tradition is consistent and uniform. As a result, there are over 250,000 differences in our current inventory of New Testament manuscripts. One of our oldest complete copies of the New Testament, the Codex Sinaiticus (4th Century), reveals the avalanche of alterations that have been introduced: academics haves counted some 14,800 modifications and margin notes that have been made or added by at least nine unknown 'correctors' over time." [23]

The discomfort and high strangeness concerning the life story of our Lord does not stop there however.

THE TALE OF THE 12 YEAR OLD JESUS

One of the New Testament's most shocking aspects is that His entire childhood, from birth on, is disregarded by the four Gospelers. Luke, and only Luke, mentions an incident in which the 12 year old Messiah visits the Jewish temple during Passover, where, due to his superior knowledge, he "astonished" the high-priests teaching there. [24] Unfortunately, Luke—who, like the other three Evangelists, was a skillful and practiced copier—seems to have "borrowed" the idea for this element from the 1ˢᵗ-Century autobiography of Josephus,[25] who writes:

> "Now, my father Matthias was not only eminent on account of his nobility, but had a higher commendation on account of his righteousness, and was in great reputation in Jerusalem, the greatest city we have. I was myself brought up with my brother, whose name was Matthias, for he was my own brother, by both father and mother; and I made mighty proficiency in the improvements of my learning, and appeared to have both a great memory and understanding. Moreover, when I was a child, and about fourteen years of age, I was commended by all for the love I had to learning; on which account the high priests and principal men of the city came then frequently to me together, in order to know my opinion about the accurate understanding of points of the law."[26]

Twelve year old Jesus at the Jerusalem Temple discoursing with the high-priests.

We will note that in describing the boy Jesus, Luke also seems to have "borrowed" from both Josephus' description of Moses[27] and the biblical description of Samuel,[28] the latter which in turn appears to have been copied from an ancient history of Samson.[29] Just as problematic: Elements in Luke's Gospel have been discovered in the pre-Lucan work *The Golden Ass*, by writer-philosopher Apuleius—obviously penned before Luke's Gospel, which is generally dated to around 180 A.D.[30]

What is more, *the first two entire chapters* of Luke's Gospel are considered late *fabricated additions* by impartial Bible scholars.[31] Luke's story of the 12 year old Jesus, pilfered from Josephus and others, is found in Chapter Two.[32]

THE 18 "SILENT YEARS" OF JESUS

Casting these particular serious issues aside for the moment, let us progress to the heart of the matter: Other than Luke's pseudo-event of the twelve year old Jesus at the temple, all four Gospelers virtually ignore Jesus' *entire* infant, childhood, adolescent, teen, young adult, and early adult years—until around the age of 29 or 30,[33] when He began His short two-three year messianic ministry before being crucified. However, to be fair to the third Evangelist, we will treat his first and second chapters (the second, as noted, which includes the plagiarized story of the adolescent Jesus), as "genuine" out of respect for traditional Christian history.

Flavius Josephus.

What remains is an intervening 18 year period (that is, from the ages of 12 to 30), a cryptic span of time that has been aptly called "the Lost Years," "the Missing Years," or "the Silent Years" of Jesus, leaving us with a suspiciously odd biblical "biography" that possesses a beginning and an end, but *no middle*. This is the equivalent of a play that possesses an opening (first) act and a closing (third) act, but lacks an all-important middle (second) act—which playwrights, screenwriters, novelists, dramatists, and librettists consider the *longest, most in-depth, and crucial act* of the three.[34]

AN UNFINISHED BIOGRAPHY

In writers' terms, this means that the biblical biography of Jesus "loses the plot" as He reaches early adolescence, just as His "character arc" is beginning to develop. As a result we do not get to see how Jesus learned the things He did, where He was educated, who taught Him, or how He acquired the skills to deal with the universal issues of relationships, work, money, and health. In short, we are not told how Jesus became the individual He eventually became: the best known, most beloved, most powerful and recognized religious figure in world history.

Reading the Bible.

To put it another way, the tumultuous developmental years spanning infancy to juvenescence, and from juvenescence to early manhood, have been either ignored or wiped from the record—in either case, a mystifying and troubling thought indeed.

If you were reading a biography of, for example, your favorite person, and it stopped at age 12 then jumped to a few years before his or her death at age 33, you would probably be quite disappointed, and rightly so. A true biography covers the entire spectrum of an individual's life, not just birth and death, but all of one's middle years, from early adolescence into adulthood, and beyond. Thus, the "biography" the four Evangelists offer us of our Lord lacks some of the most vital aspects of His life and growth as a person, as a man, as a 1st-Century Jew living in the Middle East. In literary terms, it would, in other words, be considered an incomplete or unfinished biography.

Why this large and essential piece of the life story of history's most popular individual was left out of the world's most popular book forms the foundation of our exploration of *The Greatest Jesus Mystery of All Time*, a fantastical voyage that will take us from Israel all the way to the Far East and back.

THE APOCRYPHA

Of course, the four Evangelists were Christian apologists, vindicators, and propagandists—*not* historians. Thus, their intent was not to write an authentic "History of Jesus," a detailed and historically accurate portraiture of His life from birth to death. It was to explain, defend, and champion the Christian Faith; and in this broad sense they were successful. Yet, as the only accepted "biographers" of Jesus, many details were quietly disregarded and omitted, leaving us with more questions than answers.[35]

Human nature being what it is, to fill in the glaring blank spaces left by the four canonical Gospels, fabulous stories soon began to be manufactured by highly imaginative writers during the centuries following Jesus' death, culminating in a bewildering array of what convention refers to as the Judeo-Christian "Apocrypha"—from the Greek word *apokryphos*, meaning "obscure," "secret," "to hide." This usually disparaging label is applied to ancient, Bible-related, noncanonical works, all which are considered "of dubious value," penned by "unauthorized," almost always anonymous individuals. A great many of these belong to a class of apocryphal works known as pseudepigrapha: spurious works falsely attributed to, usually, notable biblical figures, such as Daniel or Solomon.

(Note that a work can be canonical, that is, one that has been accepted into the present day Bible, and still be considered pseudepigraphal: the four Gospels and some of Paul's epistles, for example, are believed by many scholars to be anonymous works artificially attributed to others.)[36]

500 GOSPELS

Some of the better known noncanonical apocryphal works, many of them Gnostic in origin, include: the Gospel of Thomas, the Gospel of Barnabas, the Gospel of Bartholomew, the Gospel of Judas, the Secret Gospel of Mark, the Gospel of Mary, the Gospel of the Ebionites, the Gospel of the Nazaraeans, the Shepherd of Hermas, the Acts of Paul and Thecla, the Gospel of the Egyptians, and the Sophia of Jesus Christ. It has been estimated that at one time there were at least 500 gospels alone in existence, not including thousands of other apocryphal Christian works.[37]

THE INFANCY GOSPELS

Concerning our specific topic, Jesus' missing 18 years, there exists an entire series of apocryphal books known as the "Infancy Gospels," all purporting to cover the babyhood and early life of Jesus and, in some cases, his mother Mary. The three primary examples of this genre are the Infancy Gospel of Thomas, the Infancy Gospel of James, and the Gospel of the Infancy. Mainstream Christians and scholars consider such works to be fanciful—and even ludicrous—creations, manufactured sometime between the 2nd and 6th Centuries A.D.[38]

THE GOSPEL OF THOMAS

Whether one considers the Apocrypha, whatever their genre, to truly be fakes or mislabeled genuine works, I encourage my readers to investigate this problem for themselves. For example, unlike the "experts," I consider the Gospel of Thomas (not to be confused with the Infancy Gospel of Thomas) to be quite possibly authentic, and therefore a true member of the body of genuine Christian works. I touch upon this particularly important literary work in some of my other books.[39]

Ancient scroll pertaining to the Samaritans of Nablus.

A BIOGRAPHICAL CONUNDRUM

In his 1929 book *The Great Galilean*, English scholar Robert Keable made this comment about the so-called "history" of Christ:

"No man knows sufficient of the early life of Jesus to write a biography of him. For that matter, no one knows enough for the normal *Times* obituary notice of a great man. If regard were had to what we should call, in correct speech, definitely historical facts, scarcely three lines could be filled. Moreover, if newspapers had been in existence, and if that obituary notice had had to be written in the year of his death, no editor could have found in the literature of his day so much as his name. Yet few periods of the ancient world were so well documented as the period of Augustus and Tiberius. But no contemporary knew of his existence. Even a generation later, a spurious passage in Josephus, a questionable reference in Suetonius, and the mention of a name that may be his by Tacitus—that is all. His first mention in any surviving document, secular or religious, is twenty years after."[40]

WHY THE EVANGELISTS OMITTED THE SILENT YEARS

Why, we must ask, did the four Evangelists exclude the complete developmental period of Jesus' infancy, boyhood, and young adulthood, the most admired and famous religious figure in world history? Every Christian, including myself, would like to know every detail possible about the Master's life.

As I write in my book, *Seabrook's Bible Dictionary of Traditional and Mystical Christian Doctrines*:

"The Evangelists claim to be either eyewitnesses or to have gotten their information from those who were. If so, all four would certainly have known minute details about the events leading up to Jesus' birth, as well as the birth itself. How then could they not have known anything about the Master's life during the period which lay closer to their own, namely the years A.D. 12 to 30? Are we really expected to believe that nothing of interest occurred during this time, a period covering nearly a generation in the life of a man we Christians view as the most fascinating individual and most spiritually evolved soul to have ever walked the earth?

". . . The answer to these questions is elementary: the 18 Silent Years, which Catholic theologians disingenuously refer to as the 'hidden life' of Jesus, represent a purposeful omission, an intentional suppression, for His teachings must be made to look original to him so that orthodox Christianity retains its 'uniqueness,' the New Testament its 'infallibility,' the Old Testament its 'inerrantness.'[41]

THE THREAT TO DOCTRINAL INFALLIBILITY

But just what is it that would call into question the uniqueness of Jesus' teachings, as well as the infallibility of the New Testament? If Jesus' teachings are truly unique and if the New Testament is truly infallible, what is there to be afraid of? Is the orthodox

Church, conventional thinking, and the mainstream establishment hiding something? What is so threatening to its identity that formal Christianity will scarcely acknowledge it let alone debate it?

All of this leads back to my original question: Why did the four Evangelists gloss over Jesus' entire middle life, with Luke dismissing His "lost 18 years" with the vacuous statement: Jesus "was in the deserts till the day of his shewing unto Israel [at age 30]."[42] Why would the highly sociable teacher and healer spend nearly 20 years alone in the barren and unforgiving wastelands of the Middle East? Could the word "deserts" be a euphemism for a hidden truth, one so sensational that if it became public it would rock the very foundations of the organized Christian Church?

In fact, the most likely answer to all of these questions is obvious *and* widely known—and has been for 2,000 years; which is why, inevitably, it has been belittled, attacked, ignored, slandered, suppressed, and censored for at least the past 130 years ago, at which time it was first brought to light by a then little known Russian adventurer. Let us meet him.

Adoration of the three astrologers at the birth of Jesus.

Joseph, Jesus, and Mary, archetypal family unit; an ancient, mystical, Middle Eastern representation of the original prehistoric "Holy Trinity"—Christianized in the early medieval period as "the Father, the Son, and the Holy Ghost." This deeply spiritual archetype also functions as an esoteric emblem of the Hieros Gamos, which combines the sacred numbers three (male) and four (female), creating seven (enlightenment), symbolized here by Jesus (Christ consciousness). Other mystical symbolism is present as well: Joseph holds a branch of lilies, a floral symbol of spiritual illumination, spiritual rebirth, and spiritual purity; a dove hovers above Jesus, an avian symbol of love, peace, and hope; all three individuals bear a halo—also known as a nimbus or aureole—around their heads, ancient occult symbols of Theosis, that is, God in man, or self-divinity (Psalm 82:6; John 10:34, KJV).

Chapter Two

AN INTRIGUING DISCOVERY
AND ITS DISCOVERER

NOTOVITCH IN INDIA

WITH THE CONCLUSION OF OUR brief foray into the often confusing and always mystifying world of Jesus' childhood, we now arrive at the starting point of our exploration into His missing 18 years; and this begins with a man named Nikolai Notovich—more commonly known throughout English speaking countries as Nicolas Notovitch.

Notovitch, probably born around 1858, was a Victorian Russian Jew (from Crimea) who became known for his work as a journalist and explorer. In 1887, while traveling in Kashmir, a

Nicolas Notovitch.

region in India, Notovitch began to overhear intriguing oral tales about a famed ancient spiritual teacher named "Saint Issa." As Issa, pronounced EE-sha, and meaning "Lord," is a spelling variation of Isa, the Arabic name for Jesus—and as Isa is linguistically related to the sacred word-names Isha, Ishvara, Krishna, Chrishna, Christ, Iesous, Yeshua, Yehoshua, Yahweh, and Jehovah[43]—these unusual stories immediately caught the adventurer's attention.

LOCATING THE MANUSCRIPTS

Upon further inquiry Notovitch was amazed to find that there was an accepted widespread belief in the area that at the age of 13 Jesus had journeyed to and studied in the countries of Tibet, India, and

Nepal, and that chronicles of these events had been recorded in an ancient manuscript in the Pali language, translated copies (in the Tibetan language) of which were still stored in certain Tibetan monasteries. It was entitled: *Life of Saint Issa, Best of the Sons of Men.*

Having been directed specifically to a Buddhist enclave known as the Himis [Hemis] Monastery near Leh (capital city of Ladakh, India), Notovitch excitedly made his way north, anticipating a great discovery. Unfortunately, and perhaps, as an unknown foreigner, not surprisingly, upon arrival he was not allowed to view the manuscripts, and the crestfallen writer prepared for his trip back south.

The Notovitch expedition into India.

DIVINE INTERVENTION

On the way, Providence intervened, however, though in a most painful manner: While hiking over a mountainous canyon trail Notovitch slipped and fell, breaking his leg. Despite his excruciating injury, an idea occurred to him: He would return to the Himis Monastery for medical treatment and, while under the monks' care, would ask again for permission to view the secret works pertaining to the mysterious "Saint Issa."

His porters duly carried the suffering explorer back to the religious community, where, after further petitions Notovitch was finally granted—perhaps at this point out of simple compassion—access to the holy manuscript. An interpreter being summoned, the leader of the monastery read out the transcription while the now treated and recovering Notovitch carefully recorded each and every word.

THE MANUSCRIPT IN EUROPE

Elated, Notovitch then traveled to Europe with his sacred prize, seeking approval and support from the mainstream Church in publishing the manuscript. But his reception was not at all what he had expected. Orthodox Church authorities, always erring on the conservative side, were quick to dismiss him, even attempting to discourage him from putting the manuscript out in public. Historical interest was the last thing considered. To the contrary, the book was dangerous, the Church believed, and would stir up nothing but controversy, apostasy, and atheism.

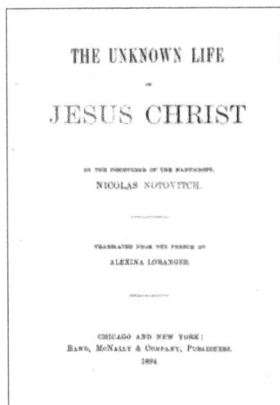

THE UNKNOWN LIFE

JESUS CHRIST

Title page of Notovitch's 1894 book, English translation.

PUBLICATION & ADVERTISING
Not one to take no for an answer, in 1894 Notovitch decided to self-publish, releasing the book that year under the provocative title, *La vie Inconnue de Jesus Christ*: "The Unknown Life of Jesus Christ."

As an example of how it was marketed to the public, twenty-eight years later, in 1922, *The Business Philosopher* magazine (Memphis, Tennessee) advertised their sale of the book like this:

"This Volume (from the pen of the noted Russian traveler, Nicholas Notovitch) is a truly remarkable book, and has created no little discussion among all classes of people.
"The original manuscript of the text is reported to have been found by him in a monastery in Thibet [Tibet], and corroborates the statements of the Great School, that Jesus was in India during the years unaccounted for in the New Testament.
"Nicholas Notovitch is the first to advance and publicly proclaim this fact, and he would seem to substantiate it by the ancient documents found in the monastery of Himes [Himis], all of which facts are now given to the World in *The Unknown Life of Jesus Christ*.
"All earnest Christians who desire, and are brave enough to learn and accept the truth, should possess this book; for it fills the hiatus existing in the Bible story of the Master, Jesus, and would seem to leave no room for doubt as to its authenticity."[44]

THE UNACCEPTED CHALLENGE
Anticipating the negative reactions he would receive from armchair "experts" and conformist mainstream commentators, in his new

book Notovitch openly exhorted the public to send designated study groups to India to research his findings for themselves. Wrote the explorer imploringly—and quite transparently:

> ". . . Before criticising my work, the learned societies could, without much expense, organize a scientific expedition, having for its mission the study of these manuscripts on the spot and thus verify their historical value."[45]

The Himis Monastery.

Unfortunately, few mainstream Christians have ever chosen to accept this forthright challenge. If they had, Notovitch's manuscript might now be included in new translations of the Bible and my book, *The Greatest Jesus Mystery of All Time*, which you now hold in your hands, would have a very different viewpoint.

PRAISE & CRITICISM
Naturally, *The Unknown Life of Jesus Christ* sparked a firestorm of interest, both positive and negative. On the latter side, in both Europe and America, Notovitch was roundly castigated by conservative theologians for perpetuating a "hoax." On the former side, he was praised by the open-minded for bringing to light an important missing element of Jesus' biography. And here it should be pointed out that while Notovitch's critics are happy to condemn him as a trickster, they do not offer any solutions to the riddle of Jesus' missing 18 years (in reality—as Luke's first two chapters are forgeries—29 to 30 years).

MY VIEW
I myself side with Notovitch, and believe that even if his work turns out to be inauthentic, this would not negate the view that Jesus once visited and studied in Central Asia. If one chooses to consider this idea false, then he or she must explain why this belief is both so

prevalent, and ubiquitous; why it can be found even today in communities from Israel and Iraq to China and Mongolia—a region covering the entire Near, Middle, and Far East, and containing over half the world's population.

THE AUTHENTICITY OF THE MANUSCRIPT

The city of Leh, India.

There are, however, even more persuasive reasons why I believe in the probable authenticity of both this view and in Notovitch's manuscript.

Several early 20th-Century individuals visited India, in part, for the express purpose of checking up on his findings. In 1922, for instance, after reading Notovitch's book, Swami Abhedananda, a noted disciple of the famed Hindu religious leader and mystic Ramakrishna Paramahansa, traveled to the Himis Monastery, where he was shown the Saint Issa manuscripts, after which he recorded and published his own translation in the Bengali language in a 1929 book entitled, *Journey Into Kashmir and Tibet*.[46]

In another example, in the 1920s, celebrated Russian archaeologist, artist, and explorer Nicholas Roerich launched an expedition to India and Tibet, where he was able to procure the same (or similar) manuscript copies that Notovitch had seen. In his 1929 book, *Heart of Asia*, Roerich writes:

"In Srinagar [India] we first encountered the curious legend about Christ's visit to this place. Afterwards we saw how widely spread in India, in Ladakh and in Central Asia, was the legend of the visit of Christ to these parts during his long absence, quoted in the Gospel. The Moslems of Srinagar told us that the crucified Christ—or, as they call him, Issa—did not die on the cross, but only lost consciousness. The disciples took away his body, secreted it and cured him. Later, Issa was taken to Srinagar, where he taught the people. And there He died. The tomb of the Teacher is in the basement of a private house. It is said that an inscription exists there stating that the son of Joseph is buried there. Near the tomb, miraculous cures are said to take place and fragrant aromas to fill the air. In this way, the people of other religions desire to have Christ among them."[47]

Roerich also came upon the story of Saint Issa in the Indian city of Leh:

"In Leh, we again encountered the legend of Christ's visit to these parts. The Hindu postmaster of Leh, and several Ladaki Buddhists told us that in Leh not far from the bazaar, there still exists a pond, near which stood an old tree. Under this tree Christ preached to the people, before his departure to Palestine. We also heard another legend of how Christ, when young, arrived in India with a merchant's caravan and how He continued to study higher wisdom in the Himalayas. We heard several versions of this legend which has spread widely throughout Ladakh, Sinkiang [Xinjiang, China] and Mongolia, but all versions agree on one point, that during the time of His absence, Christ was in India and Asia. It does not matter how and from where the legend originated. Perhaps it is of Nestorian origin. It is valuable to see that the legend is told in full sincerity."[48]

The belief that Jesus spent his 18 "lost years" in Central Asia, and perhaps in other surrounding regions, is further supported by the fact that while visiting Kashgar, an oasis city in Xinjiang, China, Roerich met up with stories about Jesus' mother Mary:

"About six miles from Kashgar is the Miriam Mazar, the so-called tomb of the Holy-Virgin, Mother of Christ. The legend relates that, after the persecution of Jesus in Jerusalem, Miriam fled to Kashgar [China], where the place of her burial is marked by a mazar, worshipped up till today."[49]

Later in his expedition, again in the town of Leh, Roerich was once more regaled with references to Asian stories about Saint Issa, this time by a Muslim:

"In the late evening, just before crossing rocky Kurul Davan, an unexpected guest visited us, an old grey-bearded Moslem. Surrounded by huge rocks before the tent, in the moonlight, we spoke about the Koran and Mahomet. He told us how Mahomet venerated womanhood. Then he spoke about the manuscripts and legends of Issa (Jesus), the best of human sons. He told us how Moslems are eager to obtain everything concerning Issa at any cost."[50]

When confronted by Notovitch's acrimonious detractors, Roerich responded:

"[During my time in India and other Asian regions, we] learned how widespread are the legends about Issa. It is important only to know the substance of these legends. The sermons related in them, of unity, of the significance of woman and all the indications about Buddhism, are so remarkably timely for us. Lamas know the significance of these legends. And why do people resent and slander these legends? Every one knows how to slander the so-called 'Apocrypha.' For slander does not need a high intelligence. *But who can fail to recognize that many of the so-called 'Apocrypha' are far more basically true than many official documents?* [my emphasis, L.S.] The Kraledvorsky manuscript which was accepted by every one happened to be a forgery—while many genuine documents do not enter into any one's consciousness.

"It is enough to remember the so-called 'Evangel of the Ebionites.' Such authorities as Origen, Jerome and Epiphany speak about the existence of this biography. Irenaeus, in the second century, knows of it—and where is it now?

"It is better, instead of useless discussions, humanly to reflect on the facts and thoughts which are communicated in the legends of Issa, 'the best of human sons.' *Appreciate how close to contemporary consciousness is the substance of these legends and be astonished how widely all the East knows of them and how persistent is the repetition of them*" [my emphasis, L.S.].[51]

MORE ENDORSEMENTS FROM EAST & WEST

The musicians of the Himis Monastery.

Aside from these very convincing cases, numerous other individuals of great repute have come forward in support of Notovitch; or, if not of Notovitch himself, at least the view that Jesus studied outside Israel during His young adulthood. Among these we have Sri Bharati Krishna Tirtha (Indian orator and mathematician), Madame Elisabeth Caspari (Swiss educator and Montessorian), William O. Douglas (U.S. Supreme Court Justice), Dr. Robert S. Ravicz (professor of anthropology, California State University), Sri Daya

Mata (female Hindu religious leader), and Edward F. Noack (American traveler and explorer).

However, in my opinion the most convincing endorsement for both Notovitch and the "Jesus-in-India" theory comes from the late Paramahansa Yogananda, a celebrated, unimpeachable, spiritually enlightened yogi and guru, as well as the founder of the highly respected Self-Realization Fellowship. Known as "the pioneering father of Yoga in the West," Yogananda is the author of a number of works, including the "spiritual classic" *Autobiography of a Yogi*. Tellingly, he devotes an entire chapter to Notovitch and the Saint Issa manuscripts in his book *The Second Coming of Christ*.

THE 2,000 YEAR OLD BELIEF THAT WILL NOT GO AWAY

Even if one dismisses the approval of these seven highly respected individuals, even if one discounts the eyewitness testimonies *and* hard evidence of Swami Abhedananda and Nicholas Roerich, and even if one discards Notovitch and his "manuscript" altogether, one thing remains: the lingering 2,000 year old belief of billions of people living in the most populous region on earth, that Jesus visited and studied topics—such as spirituality, sacred scripture, healing, philosophy, medicine, and mathematics—there between the ages of 12 and 30.

The seventh bridge of Srinagar, India.

Chapter Three

MORE EVIDENCE THAT JESUS
MAY HAVE STUDIED IN THE EAST

JESUS' MOTIVATION FOR VISITING INDIA AT AGE 12

LET US ADDRESS AN OFTEN asked question: What would motivate a 12 or 13 year old Jesus to abandon his Judean homeland and a loving family to embark on the treacherous journey across the Near and Middle East to India?

According to the Tibetan manuscripts uncovered by Notovitch, the 12 year old Jesus was soon to enter adulthood, as 13 is the period at which Jewish boys are considered to "come of age" (marked by a Bar Mitzvah ceremony). Marriage and the many responsibilities of manhood were on the horizon, and, as the brilliant and highly educated Jesus was considered to be excellent husband material, "the most noble and rich sought him as a son-in-law."[52]

Discovered in the Catacombs, this is said to be the oldest depiction of Jesus known.

As the story goes, wishing to avoid what must have seemed like a restrictive situation to the intellectually adventurous lad, and also yearning to expand his knowledge about spirituality and the world's religions, shortly after His visit to the Jerusalem Temple, Jesus ran away from home, traveling onward to India with a caravan of traders.[53]

At around the age of 29, after achieving His educational goals in South Asia, Jesus ventured back to Israel through present day Afghanistan, Iran, and Iraq, where the four Gospelers, "Matthew,"

"Mark," "Luke," and "John," once again pick up His "biography," ending the entire saga with our Lord's crucifixion and resurrection.

Hearing of His death on the cross, grief-stricken Buddhist monks, though living thousands of miles away, decided to chronicle their memories of Jesus' time with them, subsequently resulting in the manuscript that Notovitch stumbled upon in 1887.

ROERICH MAGAZINE ARTICLE

While subjective alethophobes spend their time ridiculing this story from their armchairs, objective truth-seekers go in search of evidence—out in the field. Such was the case of the aforementioned Nicholas Roerich. What follows is a 1926 magazine article by English-American journalist Thurston Macauley reporting on Roerich and his expedition to India, providing additional important details to our discussion:

ROERICH FINDS RECORDS OF CHRIST IN TIBET

"Nicholas Roerich, who has been termed, quite justly, the foremost living Russian painter, is heading an art expedition through the Himalayas, and is the first Western artist to interpret that region of magnificent scenery on his canvases, and to seek out its own native treasures. He has already sent back over a hundred paintings completed on his journey, and many of these are now beautifully reproduced in a monograph that has just been published—in an edition limited to 500 copies. This book, one of unusual interest to every art lover, will doubtless be eagerly sought by all collectors of rare works, for of the small number printed only half are on sale: the remainder have been sent to museums in this country and in Europe.

"Appreciative and interpretive accounts [concerning the] artist's life and works, by Frances D. Grant, Mary Siegrist, George Grebenstchikoff and Ivan Narodny are included in this volume, together with delightful impressions of his travels in Tibet by Roerich himself, under the [series] chapter-title, 'Banners of the East.'

"While the first exhibition of Roerich's canvases in America was held as recently as 1920, there is now a Roerich Museum in New York, which contains some 600 of his paintings, including the ones recently sent from Tibet. In addition, there are 2,500 of his canvases in museums and private collections in fourteen other countries. Thus the Russian artist's work is to be seen in nearly all the great galleries of the world—the Louvre, the Luxembourg, and the rest.

"Roerich has a strong feeling for America. As far back as twenty-five years ago he organized the first exhibition of American art in Russia, when most Europeans were still reluctant to admit the existence of such a thing as American art. He came to this country by way of London, where officials of the Chicago Art Institute saw his work and invited him to exhibit in their city. Later, he made a tour of principal cities in the United States and did a number of interesting paintings in Maine, Arizona, and New Mexico.

Nicholas Roerich.

"When he embarked on the present expedition, of which he writes in 'Banners of the East,' a definite period in the artist's life was brought to a close. While there is a monumental quality about all his earlier work in Russia, in the Himalayan canvases he reaches the apex of his achievement. In his paintings one sees his desire for a universal, world-wide religion, merging Christianity, Buddhism, Mohammedanism, and all the rest into one.

"'Banners of the East' is a remarkable account of a journey through a remarkable region, set down by an artist who absorbed its lofty inspiration. Its value is enhanced by the fact that in certain Buddhist monasteries of Tibet he found preserved the teachings of Christ, who, according to the lamas, passed through Tibet and taught there while he was still on earth. The discovery of these records of Christ sheds some light on his 'lost years': the Bible as we know, does not tell where Christ was or what he did for a period of over ten years, from his teens to his twenty-ninth year. *Roerich quotes from the Tibetan documents, which, he says, have the antiquity of about fifteen hundred years* [my emphasis, L.S.]. In them Jesus is referred to as 'Issa.' A part of them that he has transcribed in 'Banners of the East' reads:

> 'Issa secretly left his parents, and, together with the merchants of Jerusalem, turned towards India to become perfected in the Divine Word. And for the study of the laws of the Great Buddha. He passed his time in Djagernath, in Rajagriha, in Benares. All loved him because Issa dwelt in peace with Vicias and Sudras, whom he instructed.'

"The Vicias and Sudras, Roerich explains, were the working ones, the humble folk. He said that Christ, in passing through India and Tibet, did not turn 'to the Brahmins and the Kshatriyas, but to the Sudras' [i.e., the working class].

> 'Vicias and Sudras were struck with astonishment and asked what they could perform. Issa bade them "Worship not the idols. Do not consider yourself first. Do not humiliate your neighbor. Help the poor. Sustain the feeble. Do evil to no one. Do not covet that which you do not possess, but which is possest by others."
>
> 'The Brahmins and warriors, learning of the words which had been told to the Sudras, decided to kill Issa. But Issa, forewarned by the Sudras, departed from this place by night. Afterwards, when he had learned the [sacred] scrolls, Issa went into Nepal and into the Himalaya mountains. Issa had reached his twenty-ninth year when he arrived in the land of Israel.'

"One also reads of Tibetan legends that connect the paths of Buddha and Christ. Roerich relates how jealously the lamas guard these secret legends. 'It is difficult to sound them,' he says, 'because lamas, above all people, know how to guard silence. Only by means of a common language—not merely that of tongue, but also of inner understanding—can one approach their significant mysteries. One becomes convinced that every educated Gelong monk knows much. Even by his eyes, one can not guess when he agrees or inwardly laughs at you, knowing more than yourself.'

"Roerich mentions another source, historically less established, which tells about the life of Jesus in Tibet. From this document he quotes a passage telling of Christ's desire to acquaint himself with a wealth of manuscripts in a temple of teaching near Lhassa [Lhasa,

Tibet], where was the greatest sage of the East—Ming-tse. There, it is said, Christ received a warm welcome, and Ming-tse 'often conversed with Jesus about the future era and about the sacred duty accepted by the people of this century.' According to this document, 'Jesus taught in the monasteries and in the bazaars; wherever the simple people gathered, there he preached.'

". . . In conclusion, it should be said that Roerich has not, thus far, given us tangible proof of the authenticity of the Christ legends [though Roerich is said to have found the Buddhists' "Jesus-in-India" manuscripts and recorded material from them; L.S.]. What he has done, however, is to set down fragments of the lore about the Nazarene that he picked up in Tibet. How such legends arose in that remote region is a mystery worth solving. The Christian world will naturally look to the Russian artist for further light on the subject."[54]

ADDITIONAL EVIDENCE

We have numerous other pieces of evidence for the nearly worldwide view that Jesus spent His "lost years" in India and Tibet studying under various spiritual masters.

For example, there is a Buddhist monastery on the island of Sri Lanka (earlier known as Ceylon) that also possesses documents recording a visit from the Jewish Messiah. There is the fact that early Christian texts have been found among ancient Tibetan chronicles. And in India a 1st-Century coin was discovered bearing the image of Jesus. The list

The Buddha in mediation.

goes on. Adding to the evidence, we have indications that our Lord may have also visited Egypt, Iran, and Greece for the same exploratory and educational purposes.[55]

The Bible itself seems to support such claims. Some of Jesus' own words suggest that at one time He traveled the world. For instance:

"And this gospel of the kingdom shall be preached in all the world for a witness unto all nations . . ."[56]

"And the gospel must first be published among all nations."[57]

". . . and that repentance and remission of sins should be preached in his name among all nations, beginning at Jerusalem."[58]

"As long as I am in the world, I am the light of the world."[59]

Saint Paul hints at the same possibility:

"And without controversy great is the mystery of godliness: God was manifest in the flesh, justified in the Spirit, seen of angels, preached unto the Gentiles, believed on in the world, received up into glory."[60]

THE SOURCE OF JESUS' EASTERN PAGAN TEACHINGS

If Jesus did *not* spend time studying in the Orient, we are entitled to ask where He derived His East Asian spiritual beliefs specifically, all which possess an obvious and distinct Oriental Pagan flavor. He would not have been taught such concepts in Israel, not by His parents nor at the Jerusalem Temple.

JESUS & THE LAW OF ATTRACTION

We have, for instance, Jesus' teaching on the divine powers of the mind and belief, encapsulated in the pre-Christian Law of Reciprocity (or Law of Attraction):

"For truly, I say to you, if you have faith like a grain of mustard seed, you will say to this mountain, 'Move from here to there,' and it will move, and nothing will be impossible for you."[61]

"Therefore I say unto you, what things soever ye desire, when ye pray, believe that ye receive them, and ye shall have them."[62]

Some 600 years earlier this same law was taught by Buddha, who stated more elaborately:

"All that we are is the result of what we have thought: it is founded on our thoughts, it is made up of our thoughts. If a man speaks or acts with an evil thought, pain follows him, as the wheel follows the foot of the ox that draws the carriage. . . . If a man speaks or acts with a pure thought, happiness follows him, like a shadow that never leaves him. . . . It is good to tame the mind, which is difficult to hold in and flighty, rushing wherever it listeth; a tamed mind brings happiness. Let the wise man guard his thoughts, for they are difficult to perceive, very artful, and they rush wherever they list: thoughts well guarded bring happiness.

"Those who bridle their mind . . . will be free from the bonds of Mara [illusion, Satan]. If a man's thoughts are unsteady, if he does not know the true law, if his peace of mind is troubled, his knowledge will never be perfect. If a man's thoughts are not dissipated . . . then there is no fear for him while he is watchful. . . . Whatever a hater may do to a hater, or an enemy to an enemy, a wrongly-directed mind will do us greater mischief. Not a mother, not a father will do so much, nor any other relative; a well-directed mind will do us greater service."[63]

JESUS & THE DOCTRINE OF THE THIRD EYE

There is Jesus' teaching on the Hindu doctrine of the Third Eye, known in esoteric Christianity as the "Star of Bethlehem":

"The light of the body is the [third] eye: if therefore thine eye be single, thy whole body shall be full of light. But if thine eye be evil, thy whole body shall be full of darkness. If therefore the light that is in thee be darkness, how great is that darkness!"[64]

Our blessed Savior.

JESUS & THE SEVEN CHAKRAS

Knowledge of the Third Eye implies a thorough knowledge of the seven astral body energy centers known as chakras, for the Third Eye is the sixth chakra. They are located along the astral spinal cord. In order, along with their Hindu name and color, they are:

1. Root Chakra (Muladhara/red)
2. Sacra Chakra (Svadhisthana/orange)
3. Solar Plexus Chakra (Manipura/yellow)
4. Heart Chakra (Anahata/green)
5. Throat Chakra (Vishuddha/blue)
6. Third Eye Chakra (Ajna/indigo)
7. Crown Chakra (Sahasrara/violet)

If I am correct, our Lord must have been very familiar with the chakra system, which is often imaged as seven sparkling wheels, flowers, or discs.

Though most references Jesus might have made to the seven chakras would have been censored and deleted during what I call "The Great Catholic Bible Revision" (to be discussed shortly), a remnant of His chakra teachings seem to have survived in the Gnostic-influenced Book of Revelation, where He is portrayed holding "seven stars" in his right hand.[65] These seven chakra-like objects are, in turn, related to the "seven churches," another mystical reference to the seven chakras.[66] When it comes to the Bible, nearly all is symbolism, metaphor, and allegory.[67]

THE SACRED MEANING BEHIND THE NUMBER SEVEN

What is the significance of the number seven? It is related to the binary Law of Polarity, that is, of male and female energies. *Three* is the numerical symbol of the Masculine Principle (Sun/Heaven), *four* is the numerical symbol of the Feminine Principle (Moon/Earth), which, when the two are combined in sacred union (known anciently as the Hieros Gamos), equals *seven*, the numerical symbol of spiritual enlightenment (coming into consciousness); that is, Life itself. This three-fold family unit—comprising a father, a mother, and a child—represents the world's first "Holy Trinity," a truly sacred archetype that predates all religions and is found in prehistoric art many thousands of years old.[68]

JESUS & THE DOCTRINE OF REINCARNATION

Although most Christians, including myself, do not embrace the Pagan Eastern doctrine of metempsychosis or reincarnation, our Lord makes numerous references to what appears to be just that. A few examples:

> "Verily I say unto you, Among them that are born of women there hath not risen a greater than John the Baptist: notwithstanding he that is least in the kingdom of heaven is greater than he. And from the days of John the Baptist until now the kingdom of heaven suffereth violence, and the violent take it by force. For all the prophets and the law prophesied until John. And if ye will receive it, this is Elias, which was for to come. He that hath ears to hear, let him hear."[69]

"When Jesus came into the coasts of Caesarea Philippi, he asked his disciples, saying, 'Whom do men say that I the Son of man am?' And they said, 'Some say that thou art John the Baptist: some, Elias; and others, Jeremias, or one of the prophets.'"[70]

Jesus feeding the five-thousand.

"And his disciples asked him, saying, 'Why then say the scribes that Elias must first come?' And Jesus answered and said unto them, 'Elias truly shall first come, and restore all things. But I say unto you, that Elias is come already, and they knew him not, but have done unto him whatsoever they listed. Likewise shall also the Son of man suffer of them.' Then the disciples understood that he spake unto them of John the Baptist."[71]

"Jesus answered and said unto him, 'Verily, verily, I say unto thee, Except a man be born again, he cannot see the kingdom of God.' Nicodemus saith unto him, 'How can a man be born when he is old? can he enter the second time into his mother's womb, and be born?' Jesus answered, 'Verily, verily, I say unto thee, Except a man be born of water and of the Spirit, he cannot enter into the kingdom of God. That which is born of the flesh is flesh; and that which is born of the Spirit is spirit. Marvel not that I said unto thee, Ye must be born again.

The wind bloweth where it listeth, and thou hearest the sound thereof, but canst not tell whence it cometh, and whither it goeth: so is every one that is born of the Spirit.'[72]

"Your father Abraham rejoiced to see my day: and he saw it, and was glad." Then said the Jews unto him, "Thou art not yet fifty years old, and hast thou seen Abraham?" Jesus said unto them, "Verily, verily, I say unto you, Before Abraham was, I am."[73]

The Master Teacher going about His "Father's business."

"And as Jesus passed by, he saw a man which was blind from his birth. And his disciples asked him, saying, 'Master, who did sin, this man, or his parents, that he was born blind?' Jesus answered, 'Neither hath this man sinned, nor his parents: but that the works of God should be made manifest in him.'"[74]

"I am the door: by me if any man enter in, he shall be saved, and shall go in and out, and find pasture."[75]

"Let not your heart be troubled: ye believe in God, believe also in me. In my Father's house are many mansions: if it were not so, I would have told you. I go to prepare a place for you. And if I go and prepare a place for you, I will come again, and receive you unto myself; that where I am, there ye may be also."[76]

JESUS & THE PHILOSOPHY OF YOGA

Not surprisingly, Jesus also alludes to the Hindu and Buddhist art and science of yoga, saying:

"Come to me, all you who are weary and burdened, and I will give you rest. Take my yoke [*zeugos*] upon you and learn from me, for I am gentle and humble in heart, and you will find rest for your souls. For my yoke [*zeugos*] is easy and my burden is light."[77]

To understand this statement let us note that: 1) in English the Greek word *zeugos* can be spelled either "yoke" or "yoga"; and 2) in fact, the word yoga means "to yoke, join, or unite." Thus, in this passage Jesus is actually saying, "my yoga is easy."

Jesus walking on water.

JESUS & THE PRACTICE OF MEDITATION

Jesus taught the Buddhistic art form of meditation, as is clear from the following scripture:

> "But thou, when thou prayest, enter into thy closet, and when thou hast shut thy door, pray to thy Father which is in secret; and thy Father which seeth in secret shall reward thee openly."[78]

JESUS & THE DOCTRINE OF THEOSIS

Jesus also taught the Hindu philosophy of theosis, that is, "God in man":

> "I and my Father are one." Then the Jews took up stones again to stone him. Jesus answered them, "Many good works have I shewed you from my Father; for which of those works do ye stone me?" The Jews answered him, saying, "For a good work we stone thee not; but for blasphemy; and because that thou, being a man, makest thyself God." Jesus answered them, "Is it not written in your law, I said, '*Ye are gods*'? If he called them gods, unto whom the word of God came, and the scripture cannot be broken; Say ye of him, whom the Father hath sanctified, and sent into the world, 'Thou blasphemest'; because I said, I am the Son of God? If I do not the works of my Father, believe me not. But if I do, though ye believe not me, believe the works: that ye may know, and believe, that the Father is in me, and I in him."[79]

JESUS & THE DOCTRINE OF THE GREAT I AM

Another aspect of the Pagan Eastern doctrine of theosis, that is, personal divinity, which Jesus taught involves the Great "I AM," also written "Aum," "Om," and "Amun" in Asia and Africa, and "Amen" in the West. This concept appears most prominently in the Old Testament in a discussion between Moses and God:

> And Moses said unto God, "Behold, when I come unto the children of Israel, and shall say unto them, 'The God of your fathers hath sent me unto you'; and they shall say to me, 'What is his name?' what shall I say unto them?" And God said unto Moses, "I AM THAT I AM": and he said, "Thus shalt thou say unto the children of Israel, I AM hath sent me unto you."[80]

In plain English I AM THAT I AM means "I am what I will to be," a statement that touches on numerous other Pagan Eastern concepts besides theosis. These would include the Law of the Mind, the Law of Attraction, the Law of Faith and Belief, the Law of Healing, and the Law of Verbal Manifestation. The God-man Jesus, with whom, according to Him, you and I are one,[81] repeatedly used the Great I AM, or Om, statement throughout His ministry.

Theosis: "Ye are gods," said Jesus (John 10:34), quoting the Old Testament (Psalm 82:6).

As I lay out in my book *Jesus and the Law of Attraction*,[82] what follows are a number of biblical examples. Note that if you would like to understand the *inner meaning* of these utterances (as Jesus intended for the spiritually mature, that is, those "with eyes to see"), rather than the superficial literal meaning used by convention, as you read them substitute the phrase "Spiritual Law is" for "I AM":

"I AM from above."[83]
"I AM the bread of life."[84]
"I AM the door of the sheep."[85]
"I AM the good shepherd."[86]
"I AM the light of the world."[87]
"I AM he that liveth."[88]
"I AM Master and Lord."[89]
"I AM meek and lowly in heart."[90]
"I AM a king."[91]
"I AM the way, the truth, and the life."[92]
"I AM the true vine."[93]
"I AM the Christ."[94]

JESUS & THE DOCTRINE OF THE DIVINE FEMININE

Though Jesus preached countless Hindu, Buddhist, Tibetan, and Egyptian doctrines, let us look at just one more example: the philosophy of the Divine Feminine—which our Savior variously referred to as "love," the "Comforter," and the "Holy Ghost":

> " Master, which is the great commandment in the law?" Jesus said unto him, "Thou shalt love the Lord thy God with all thy heart, and with all thy soul, and with all thy mind. This is the first and great commandment. And the second is like unto it, Thou shalt love thy neighbour as thyself. On these two commandments hang all the law and the prophets."[95]

> "But the Comforter, which is the Holy Ghost, whom the Father will send in my name, he shall teach you all things, and bring all things to your remembrance, whatsoever I have said unto you."[96]

The Virgin Mary enveloped in the Sun's rays, wearing a crown of 12 stars (representing the 12 astrological sun-signs), and sitting on a crescent Moon (symbol of the Divine Feminine)—Pagan iconography borrowed from the Hindu solar-deity Aditi, goddess of motherhood. See Revelation 12:1.

JESUS & THE HINDU LAW OF KARMA

The Master was also knowledgeable in the ancient Hindu doctrine of karma (cause and effect), possessing a perfect understanding that how we think, what we believe, what we say and do, *always* comes back to us—which is why, for example, He laid so much stress on attributes such as forgiveness.[97] Thus asserted Jesus:

". . . all who draw the sword will die by the sword."[98]

Srinagar, India, one of the many Eastern cities where Jesus is said to have taught the masses, and where the story of His travels across Central Asia thrives to this day.

JESUS & ANCIENT HINDU SCRIPTURES

Finally, we must take into account the fact that many of Jesus' teachings and doctrines, if not His exact wording in numerous instances, come from Eastern Pagan texts, an intriguing example being the Hindu's Khandogya-Upanishad. One of its passages concerns mystical doctrines, which cannot be directly transmitted to the rational literalistic mind (tuition), but which must instead come from the God Within (intuition)—which Jesus sometimes referred to as the "Heavenly Father." This is a type of occult (inner) instruction, the Upanishad states,

"by which we hear what cannot be heard, by which we perceive what cannot be perceived, by which we know what cannot be known."[99]

Centuries later Jesus made the following comment to His initiates (the Apostles) when they asked Him why He taught His ordinary followers using mystical concepts (for example, parables) instead of clearly and openly, to which He replied:

> "That seeing they may see and not perceive; and hearing they may hear and not understand."[100]

JESUS & THE BHAGAVAD GITA

Another one of Jesus' favorite sacred Eastern texts seems to have been the awe-inspiring work known as the Bhagavad Gita ("Song of the Lord"), which contains a conversation between the Hindu Savior Chrishna (that is, Krishna) and his devotee, the warrior-hero Arjuna.

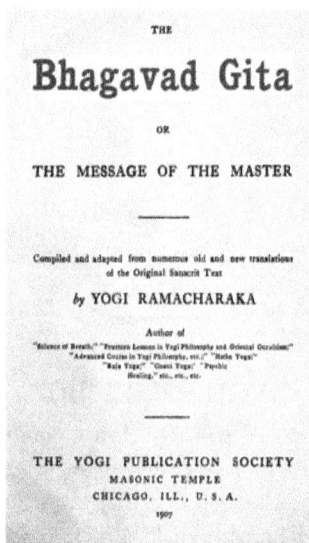

THE

Bhagavad Gita

OR

THE MESSAGE OF THE MASTER

Compiled and adapted from numerous old and new translations
of the Original Sanscrit Text

by YOGI RAMACHARAKA

Author of
"Science of Breath," "Fourteen Lessons in Yogi Philosophy and Oriental Occultism,"
"Advanced Course in Yogi Philosophy, etc.," "Hatha Yoga,"
"Raja Yoga," "Gnani Yoga," "Psychic
Healing," etc., etc., etc.

THE YOGI PUBLICATION SOCIETY
MASONIC TEMPLE
CHICAGO, ILL., U. S. A.
1907

Title page of an edition of the Bhagavad Gita, from my personal library.

In studying the Gita over the years I have discovered a striking number of similarities between the words and doctrines (not to mention the names) of the *pre-Christian* Chrishna and Christ,[101] a partial list which follows. For instance:

> Chrishna: "Those who worship me devoutly dwell in me and I in them."[102]
> Christ: "I am in my Father, and ye in me, and I in you."[103]

Chrishna: "Rest assured that they who worship me never perish."[104]
Christ: "Verily, verily I say unto you, he that believeth on me hath everlasting life."[105]

Chrishna: "By knowing . . . thou wilt be delivered from misfortune."[106]
Christ: "And ye shall know the truth, and the truth shall make you free."[107]

Chrishna: "The Yogi of a subdued mind, thus employed in the exercise of his devotion, is compared to a lamp, standing in a place without wind, which flickereth not."[108]
Christ: "Let your light so shine before men, that they may see your good works, and glorify your Father which is in heaven."[109]

Chrishna: "I AM the producer and the destroyer of the whole universe. . . . I AM the beginning, the middle, and also the end of all beings."[110]
Christ: "I AM Alpha and Om-ega, the beginning and the end, the first and last."[111]

Chrishna: "I AM [the] taste in the [living] waters."[112]
Christ: "He that believeth on me [that is, the universal I AM] . . . out of his belly shall flow rivers of living water."[113]

JESUS & THE GOSPEL OF THE KINGDOM OF GOD

Many other such examples could be listed, all of which Jesus preserved in the gospel that He Himself used and taught: "The Gospel of the Kingdom," or more fully, "The Gospel of the Kingdom of God"[114]—which our Lord mystically taught is "within you."[115]

Tragically, sometime during the formation of the orthodox Christian Church (1st to 5th Centuries) Jesus' Gospel of the Kingdom of God was suppressed and expelled from the Bible, replaced with the "churchianity" version known today as "The Gospel of Jesus Christ."[116] In this way, Christianity went from a religion centered on the message to one focused on the messenger.[117] But worse was to come.

THE GREAT CATHOLIC BIBLE REVISION

By the time of the formalization of the Bible canon in the late 4th Century A.D., the highly educated Catholic hierarchy—well-versed in philosophy and world religions, was already acutely aware of the Paganism behind Jesus' words. Inevitably, this is what led, in great part I believe, to a major rewriting of the Bible around this time (circa 5th Century), and in particular the New Testament, which was thoroughly "worked over" by priestly scribes in order to "cleanse" it of any and all obvious connections between Christ and non-Christian doctrines. By the time of the reign of the religious totalitarian, Pope Theodosius I (6th Century A.D.), what I call "The Great Catholic Bible Revision" was nearly complete, with many of Jesus' original sayings, teachings, and doctrines either missing or having undergone an appallingly dramatic change in tone, form, and content.[118]

Jesus preached a spiritual doctrine called "The Gospel of the Kingdom of God." What happened to it?

Despite this intense centuries-long effort to "scrub" the Bible clean, a number of the Messiah's original statements, or at least traces of their inner meanings, along with hints of their pre-Christian Pagan origins and connections, were preserved in the Bible (as well as in ancient works such as the Gospel of Thomas and the Secret Gospel of Mark)—as this entire chapter amply demonstrates.[119]

JESUS: AN ORIENTAL CHRIST

One should not be surprised if Jesus did in fact derive many of His teachings and ideas from the Far East: Jesus was a Jew born in the East (the "Orient"), and was thus an Oriental Christ, making both the Bible and Christianity themselves Eastern or Oriental in origin and character.[120]

"The clergy would censor the Bible." Caption and illustration from a 1917 book.

Why then should it be a shock to learn that there is an ancient and well documented tradition that during His "Silent Years," our Lord not only studied and taught (and perhaps lived) at the great Essene Community at Qumran near the Dead Sea, but that He also journeyed throughout the Mideast, primarily India, Tibet, Nepal, Persia, the Ladakh region, and Arabia, both learning and instructing under the tutelage of various spiritual masters, including the Pythagoreans, the Essenes, and the Gnostics.[121]

JESUS & THE BANNED BOOK OF ENOCH

For those who still doubt that our Lord would study, quote, and teach banned Judeo-Christian, or even non-Judeo-Christian (Pagan), doctrines and beliefs, let us harken back to our previous discussion on the Apocrypha.

One of the more famous Judeo-Christian apocryphal works is the Book of Enoch, which, early on, was banned from the Bible. Yet, it happened to be one of Jesus' favorite ancient works of literature. Indeed, not only did He obviously study it assiduously, He both endorsed and taught its doctrines—just as did His brother Jude, Saint Paul, and many of the early Church Fathers. For example, Jesus paraphrases it on

The Bible states that Enoch lived "365 years" (Genesis 5:23), a mystical reference to his original function as a Sun-god—as this 18th-Century artwork overtly illustrates.

numerous occasions (His sibling Jude went further, quoting it verbatim), while it is said that Paul carried the Book of Enoch with him wherever he went, using it as a sort of pocket reference. What is more, the earliest Fathers—important Church leaders such as Barnabas, Athenagoras, Clement of Alexandria, Irenaeus, and Tertullian—accepted it as literal valid scripture.[122]

What follows are just two instances in which Jesus' dependence on the Book of Enoch can be clearly seen:

Enoch: "The elect shall possess light, joy and peace, and they shall inherit the earth."[123]

Jesus: "Blessed are the meek, for they shall inherit the earth."[124]

Enoch: "Woe to you who are rich, for in your riches have you trusted; but from your riches you shall be removed."[125]

Jesus: "Woe unto you that are rich! for ye have received your consolation."[126]

BOOK & GOSPEL BANNING IN THE EARLY CHURCH

Jesus reassuring his Disciples: "I will pray the Father, and he shall give you another Comforter, that he may abide with you forever" (John 14:16).

Once again, we must ask: Why was one of Jesus' favorite books censored and tossed in the "trash heap" that the orthodox still disdainfully refer to as the "Apocrypha"? Why was a book that was admired and quoted by our Lord and His family, and even accepted as authentic and divinely inspired by the earliest Church Fathers, eventually banished and censored?[127]

For the same reason both Jesus' Gospel of the Kingdom of God and the story of His youthful sojourn into the Far East (between the ages of 12 and 30) were prohibited and finally suppressed: *To hide the fact that many of the most famous and beloved doctrines taught by Christ, and in turn later by the Church, were not original to Him, and thus were not uniquely Christian, but were in fact Hebraic, Gnostic, Essenic, or even fully Pagan, in origin.*[128]

Thus, by the 4th Century, when the fact was finally realized that the Book of Enoch undermined the uniqueness and infallibility of orthodox Christianity, the Church callously barred the work from the canon under such Fathers as Hilary, Jerome, and Augustine. It then went out of circulation and became one of the Bible's many "lost books," relegated to the apocryphal garbage dump alongside the story of Jesus' "lost years."[129]

Fortunately for you and I, and more importantly for history itself, the "lost" Book of Enoch was rediscovered in 1947 in Israel as part of the great Essene Library (deceptively known as the "Dead Sea Scrolls"), while the "lost" Book of the *Life of Saint Issa* was eventually recovered in 1887 in India by Notovitch.[130] I believe that all thinking Christians should be thankful to God for these miracles.[131]

In a world filled with ignorant egoists, self-centered know-it-alls, and narcissistic authoritarians imprisoned behind a wall of confirmation bias, book banning is nothing new. These intolerant, dull-minded, dogmatic individuals are the same ones who participated in the ancient and tragic destruction of the great Library at Alexandria, Egypt—one of the largest and most important centers of knowledge the world has ever known. These are identical to the "experts" Jesus accused of "taking away the key of [esoteric] knowledge" (Luke 11:52). As Albert Einstein once said: "Great spirits have always encountered violent opposition from mediocre minds."

French map showing Notovitch's itinerary across India.

Chapter Four

NOTOVITCH ON THE BUDDHIST
MANUSCRIPT OF SAINT ISSA (JESUS)

NOW THAT WE HAVE TOUCHED on the basics surrounding the worldwide belief that Jesus spent His young adulthood in Asia, let us take a more penetrating and in-depth look into the details of the story itself. In order to do so we will turn to Notovitch, who was a firsthand eyewitness to the Buddhist manuscripts pertaining to Saint Issa, whom we know now as Jesus. According to the Russian explorer, writing in 1894:

"In reading the life of Issa (Jesus Christ), we are at first struck by the similarity between some of its principal passages and the biblical narrative; while, on the other hand, we also find equally remarkable contradictions, which constitute the difference between the Buddhist version and that found in the Old and New Testaments.

"To explain this singularity, we must take into account the periods in which the facts were recorded.

"In childhood, we were taught to believe that the Pentateuch was written by Moses himself; but the careful investigations of contemporary savants have conclusively demonstrated, that in the days of Moses, and even long after him, there existed no writings in those countries bathed by the Mediterranean, save the Egyptian hieroglyphics and the cuneiform inscriptions still found in the excavations of Babylon. But we know, to the contrary, that the alphabet and parchment were known and used in China and India long before Moses.

"Of this we have ample proof.

Notovitch (right) and one of his porters (left) in the mountains of India.

"The sacred books of the 'religion of the wise men,' teaches us that the alphabet was invented in China, in 2800 B.C., by Fou-si, who was the first Chinese emperor to embrace that religion [Foism]. It was he who also arranged the ritual and outward ceremonies. Yaou, the fourth Chinese emperor who adopted the same faith, published moral and civil laws, and, in the year 2228 B.C., prepared a penal code.

"On his accession to the throne, Soune, the fifth emperor, proclaimed the "religion of the wise men" as the religion of state; and in 2282 B.C., he enacted new penal laws. These laws, modified by the Emperor Woo-Wang, who was the founder of the Chow dynasty in 1122 B.C., are now known under the name of the "Changes."

"Moreover, the doctrine of Buddha-Fo, whose real name was Cakya-Mouni, was written on parchment. Foism began to spread through China about the year 260 B.C.; in 206 B.C., an emperor of the Tsine dynasty, who desired to study Buddhism, sent to India for the Buddhist Silifan; while the Emperor Ming-Ti, of the Han dynasty, one year before Christ, procured the sacred books written by Cakya-Mouni, the founder of Buddhism, who lived about the year 1200 before Christ.

"The doctrine of Buddha Gaouthama, or Gautama, who lived six hundred years before Christ, was written on parchment in the Pali language. At this epoch, there already existed in India about eighty-four thousand Buddhist manuscripts, the compiling of which must have required a considerable number of years.

"While the Chinese and Hindoos already possessed a rich collection of written literature, the less fortunate, or more ignorant nations, who had no alphabet, transmitted orally, from generation to generation, what came to pass. Owing to the unreliability of the human memory, and its relative incapacity, not to speak of oriental embellishments, historical facts soon degenerated into fabulous legends, which, later, were gathered by unknown compilers and given to the world under the title of the "Five Books of Moses." The legend also attributes a truly extraordinary divine power to this Hebrew legislator, and credits him with a series of miracles performed in the presence of Pharaoh; might it not be equally mistaken in declaring that he was an Israelite by birth?

Young people in wedding attire, Ladakh, India.

"The Hindoo chroniclers, on the contrary, thanks to the invention of the alphabet, were enabled to preserve, not fabulous legends, but a concise narrative of recent events accomplished in their midst, as well as of the reports received from the merchants who had just visited foreign lands.

"It is necessary to remark here that during this period of

antiquity, as in our own days, oriental public life was concentrated in the bazaars, where the events of the day and the news from foreign nations were propagated by caravans of merchants, who were usually followed by a number of dervishes who readily told all they had seen and heard on their journey, in exchange for food. In fact, this was their sole means of subsistence.

A group of Tibetan lamas.

"The commerce of India with Egypt, and later with Europe, was carried on through Jerusalem, where, even as early as the reign of Solomon, Hindoo caravans brought precious metals and all that was necessary for the construction of the temple. From Europe, the merchandise came to Jerusalem by sea, and was unloaded in the harbor where Jaffa [Israel] now stands.

"The chronicles in question were written before, during, and after Christ; although no attention was paid to Jesus during his sojourn in India, where he came as a simple pilgrim to study the Brahman and Buddhist laws.

"But later, when the events which had aroused Israel were related in India, these chroniclers—after having committed to writing all they had just heard concerning the prophet Issa, whom an oppressed nation had followed and who had been executed by the order of Pilate—remembered that this same Issa had recently lived among them and studied in their midst, and that he had then returned to his own country. A deep interest was immediately aroused concerning this man who had so rapidly grown in importance in their eyes, and they at once began an investigation into his birth, his past, and every detail of his existence.

"*The two manuscripts read to me by the lama of the Himis Convent, were compiled from divers copies written in the Tibetan tongue, translated from rolls belonging to the Lassa library and brought from India, Nepal, and Maghada [India] two hundred years after Christ. These were placed in a convent standing on Mount Marbour, near Lassa [Lhasa, Tibet], where the Dalai-Lama now resides* [my emphasis, L.S.].

"These rolls were written in the Pali tongue, which certain lamas study carefully that they may translate the sacred writings from that language into the Tibetan dialect.

"The chroniclers were Buddhists belonging to the sect of Buddha Gautama.

"*The information contained about Christ is oddly mixed, without relation or coherence with other events of that period* [my emphasis, L.S.].

"Without preliminary details or explanation, the manuscript begins by announcing that, in the very year of the death of Christ, a few merchants just returned from Judea have brought back the information that a just man named Issa, an Israelite, after having been twice acquitted by his judges—as was the man of God—was finally put to death at the instigation of the Pagan Governor, Pilate, who feared that Jesus would take advantage of his popularity to reestablish the Kingdom of Israel and expel its conquerors from the land.

"Then comes the somewhat incoherent tale of Jesus preaching among the Guebers and other pagans, evidently written in the year following the death of Christ, in whom there is a growing interest. In one of these the merchants relate what is known of the origin of Jesus and of his family, while another gives the story of the expulsion of his partisans and the bitter persecutions they endured.

"It is not until the end of the second volume is reached, that we find the first categorical affirmation of the chronicler where he declares that Issa is blessed by God and the best of all men; that he is the chosen one of the great Brahma, the man in whom is incarnated the spirit detached from the Supreme Being at a period determined by fate.

The Vale of Kashmir.

"Having explained that Issa was the son of poor parents and of Israelite extraction, the chronicler makes a slight digression with the object of telling us who were the children of Israel.

"These fragments of the life of Issa, I have disposed of in chronological order, endeavoring to give them a character of unity totally wanting in the original form.

"I leave to savants, philosophers, and theologians, the task of searching the cause of contradictions that may be found between the "Unknown Life of Issa," which I make public, and the story told by the Evangelists. But I am inclined to believe that nobody will hesitate to acknowledge that *this version, recorded within three or four years after the death of Christ from the testimonies of eyewitnesses* [my emphasis, L.S.], is more likely to bear the stamp of truth than the narratives of *the Evangelists, who wrote at divers epochs, and so long a time after these events took place, that we can not be astonished if the facts have been altered or distorted* [my emphasis, L.S.].

"Before taking up the life of Jesus, I must say a few words concerning the history of Moses, who, according to the usually accepted legend, was an Israelite. This fact is flatly contradicted by Buddhists. We are first told that Moses was a prince of Egypt, son of Pharaoh, and that he was merely instructed by the learned Israelites. By carefully examining this important point, we are forced to admit that the Buddhist author may be right.

"Although I have no intention to destroy the biblical legend on the origin of Moses, many will concur with me in the opinion that Moses was not a simple Israelite, for the very appreciable reason that his education was that of a prince of the land; and it is difficult to believe that a child brought by chance into the palace, could have been placed on a footing of equality with the son of the sovereign. The manner in which the Egyptians treated their slaves proves that they were not distinguished for mildness of character. A foundling would assuredly not have been tolerated among the children of Pharaoh, but would have been placed with the servants. Besides, and this is preponderating evidence, we must take into consideration the spirit of caste so strictly observed in ancient Egypt.

"On the other hand, it is difficult to believe that Moses did not receive a complete education. How otherwise could we explain his great work of legislation, his broad views, and his high qualities as administrator?

"But, if he were a prince, why did he join the Israelites? The explanation is simple enough. We know that among the ancients, as well as in our modern days, the succession to the throne was frequently a bone of contention among brothers. Why not admit the hypothesis that Mossa, or Moses, wished to found a distinct kingdom, since the existence of an elder brother debarred him from the Egyptian throne? This consideration probably led him to place himself at the head of the Israelites, whom he admired for their firmness in their belief, as well as for their bodily strength. The Israelites of Egypt, we know, did not at all resemble their descendants physically, the blocks of granite used in building the palaces and the pyramids still stand as evidence of this.

"The miracles performed in the presence of Pharaoh may be explained in the same way.

"Without possessing definite arguments to deny these miracles performed by Moses, in the name of God, we must admit—without much difficulty, I believe—that the Buddhist verses are more plausible than the biblical paraphrase. The pest, small-pox, or cholera, must, in fact, have wrought terrible ravages in the dense mass of the population at a time when ideas on hygiene were still rudimentary, and when, in consequence, the scourge must have rapidly assumed frightful proportions.

The city of Leh, India, as seen from the market-place.

"Moses, who was of quick intelligence, could readily work on the fears of Pharaoh in the presence of this imminent danger, by declaring that it was due to the intervention of the God of Israel in favor of his chosen people.

"This was a most favorable opportunity to free the Israelites from their bondage and make them pass under his own power.

"Conformably to the will of Pharaoh, still, according to the Buddhists, Moses led the Israelites beyond the walls of the city; but, instead of building a new city at a certain distance from the capital, as he had been commanded to do, he took them out of the Egyptian territory. The indignation of Pharaoh on seeing Moses' utter disregard of his orders can be easily imagined; and it is not therefore astonishing if he started in pursuit of the fugitives at the head of his soldiers. Taking into consideration the geographical situation of that region, it must be supposed that Moses traveled along the mountains and entered Arabia through the isthmus now cut by the Suez Canal. Pharaoh, on the contrary, led his troops in a more direct line in the direction of the Red Sea; then, to overtake the Israelites who had already gained the opposite shore, he boldly took advantage of the ebb of the sea into the gulf formed by the banks of the isthmus, and made his soldiers march through the shallow passage. But the distance across being much longer than he had anticipated, the flood-tide caught the Egyptian army in the very middle of the sea and not one of them could escape death.

"This fact, so simple in itself, was transformed into a religious legend in the succeeding centuries by the Israelites, who interpreted the incident as due to divine intervention in their favor and as a just punishment from the hands of God on their persecutors. We are led to believe, moreover, that Moses himself entertained this belief. But this is a thesis which I shall endeavor to develop in a future work.

"The Buddhist chronicle then briefly describes the

greatness and the downfall of the kingdom of Israel, as well as its conquest by strangers who reduced its inhabitants to a state of servitude.

"The misfortunes that poured upon the Israelites and the afflictions that thereafter embittered their days, were, according to the chronicler, more than sufficient reasons for God to look with pity upon his people; and, wishing to come to their assistance, he resolved to descend upon earth under the guise of a prophet, that he might lead them back into the path of salvation.

"The condition of things at that period therefore justified the belief that the coming of Jesus was signaled, imminent, and necessary.

The inscription in the Himis Monastery.

Solomon's Throne.

"This explains why the Buddhist traditions declare that the Eternal Spirit detached itself from the Eternal Being and was incarnated in the new-born child of a pious and noble family.

"The Buddhists, no doubt, as well as the Evangelists, wish to indicate thereby that the child belonged to the royal house of David; but the text of the Gospel, according to which the 'child was conceived by the Holy Ghost,' may be interpreted in two ways, while, according to the doctrine of Buddha, which is more in conformity with the laws of nature, the Spirit incarnated itself in a child that was already born, whom God blessed and chose to accomplish his mission here below.

"*At this point there is a void in the traditions of the*

Evangelists, who, whether through ignorance or negligence, tell us nothing of his infancy, his youth, and his education. They begin the history of Jesus by his first sermon, that is when, at the age of thirty, he returned to his own country.

"All that is said by the Evangelists in regard to the infancy of Jesus is totally void of precision: 'And the child grew, and waxed strong in spirit, filled with wisdom; and the grace of God was upon him,' says one of the sacred authors, St. Luke, and again: 'And the child grew, and waxed strong in spirit, and was in the deserts till the day of his shewing unto Israel' [my emphasis, L.S.].

The women of Ladakh, India.

"As the Evangelists compiled their works long after the death of Jesus, it is presumed that they merely consigned to writing the narratives that had come to them of the principal events of the life of Jesus.

"The Buddhists, however, who compiled their chronicles immediately after the Passion, and who had the advantage of gathering the most accurate information on all points that interested them, give us a complete and exhaustive description of the life of Jesus [my emphasis, L.S.].

"In those unhappy days, when the struggle for existence seems to have destroyed all notion of God, the people of

Israel were bowed down under the double oppression of the ambitious Herod, and of the avaricious despotic Romans. Then, as now, the Hebrews placed all their hope in Providence, which, they believed, would send them the inspired man who was to deliver them from their physical and moral sufferings. Time passed on, however, and no one took the initiative in a revolt against the tyranny of the governing power.

"During this period of anxiety and hope, the people of Israel completely forgot that there existed in their midst a poor Israelite, who was a direct descendant of their King David. This poor man [Joseph] married a young girl [Mary] who gave birth to a miraculous child [Jesus].

Indian art.

"Faithful to their traditions of devotion and respect for the race of their kings, the Hebrews, on hearing of this, flocked to see the child and congratulate the happy father. It is evident that Herod did not long remain in ignorance of what had taken place; and he feared that when the child had grown to manhood, he might take advantage of his popularity to regain the throne of his ancestors. He, therefore, sought the child, whom the Israelites endeavored to shield from the anger of the king; the latter then ordered the abominable massacre of children, hoping that Jesus might perish in this vast human hecatomb. But the family of Joseph, having obtained information of the terrible execution contemplated by Herod, fled into Egypt.

"And the child [Jesus] grew, and waxed strong, filled with wisdom: and the grace of God was upon him" (Luke 2:40).

"Some time later the family returned to its native land. The child had grown during these journeys in which his life had been more than once exposed. Then as now, the Oriental Israelites commenced to instruct their children at the age of five or six years. Forced to remain in concealment, the parents never allowed their son to leave their roof, and the latter no doubt spent his time in studying the sacred writings, so that on his return to Judea, he was far in advance of the boys of his own age, which greatly astonished the learned men. He was then in his thirteenth year, the age at which, according to the Jewish law, a young man attains his majority and has the right to marry, as well as to fulfill his religious duties on an equal footing with adults.

"There still exists an ancient religious custom among the Israelites which fixes the majority of a man at the age of thirteen, when the youth enters society and enjoys the full privileges of his elders. His marriage at this age is considered absolutely legal and indispensable, even, in warm countries. In Europe, however, this custom has fallen into desuetude and lost its importance, owing to local laws, as well as to the laws of nature, which do not hasten physical development to the same degree as in warmer countries.

"His royal origin, his rare intelligence, and the extensive studies to which he had applied himself, caused him to be looked upon as an excellent suitor, and the most noble and rich sought him as a son-in-law. So the Israelites of our days seek the honor of marrying their daughters to the son of a rabbi or a learned man. *But the studious youth, seemingly detached from all things corporal and devoured by a thirst for knowledge, stealthily left his father's house and fled to India with a departing caravan* [my emphasis, L.S.].

"It is to be supposed that Jesus Christ chose India, first, because Egypt made part of the Roman possessions at that period, and then because an active trade with India had spread marvelous reports in regard to the majestic character and inconceivable riches of art and science in that wonderful country, where the aspirations of civilized nations still tend in our own age.

"Here the Evangelists again lose the thread of the terrestrial life of Jesus. St. Luke says: 'He was in the desert till the day of his shewing unto Israel,' which conclusively proves that no one knew where the young man had gone, to so suddenly reappear sixteen years later.

"Once in India, the country of marvels, Jesus began by frequenting the temples of the Djainites.

"And Jesus advanced in wisdom and stature, and in favor with God and men" (Luke 2:52).

"There still exists in the peninsula of Hindoostan [Hindustan] a sect which bears the name of Djainism; it forms a link, as it were, between Buddhism and Brahmanism, and preaches the destruction of all other beliefs, which they declare to be steeped in error. It dates back to the seventh century before Christ, and its name is derived from the word 'djaine' (conquering), which it assumes as a symbol of its triumph over its rivals.

"Amazed at the young man's wonderful intellect, the Djainites begged him to remain in their midst; but Jesus left them to settle at Juggernaut, one of the principal cities of the Brahmans, and enjoying great religious importance at the time of Christ, where he devoted himself to the study of treatises on religion, philosophy, etc. A cherished tradition claims that the ashes of the illustrious Brahman Krichna [who is today known as Veda Vyasa] are preserved here in the hollow of a tree near a magnificent temple visited by thousands every year. Krichna is supposed to have lived 1580 [years] before Christ, and it was he who gathered and arranged the Vedas, dividing the work into four books: Richt, Jagour, Saman, and Artafan. This celebrated Brahman, who in recognition of this work received the name of Viassa (he who has gathered and divided the Vedas), also compiled the Vedantha [Vendanta] and eighteen Pouranas [Puranas], composed of four hundred thousand strophes.

Jesus blessing the little children.

The Hindu Supreme Being, Brahma.

"A library, rich in Sanscrit [Sanskrit] books and precious religious manuscripts, is also found at Juggernaut.

"Jesus spent six years at this place, studying the language of the country and the Sanscrit tongue, which enabled him to dive deeply into all religious doctrines, philosophy, medicine, and mathematics. He found much to condemn in Brahman laws and customs, and entered into public debates with the Brahmans, who strove to convince him of the sacred character of their established customs. Among other things, Jesus particularly censured the injustice of humiliating the laborer, and of not only depriving him of the benefits to come, but also of contesting his right to hear religious readings. And Jesus began to preach to the Soudras [Sudras], the lowest caste of slaves, saying that God is one, according to their own laws, that all that is, exists through him, that all are equal in his sight, and that the [polytheistic] Brahmans had obscured the great principle of monotheism in perverting the words of Brahma himself and insisting to excess on the exterior ceremonies of the religion.

"These are the terms, according to the Brahman doctrine, in which God speaks of himself to the angels:

'I have been since all eternity and shall be eternally. I am the first cause of all that exists in the East and in the West, in the North and in the South, above and below, in heaven and in hell. I am older than all things. I am the Spirit and the creation of the universe and its creator. I am all-mighty, I am the God of gods, the King of kings; I am Para-Brahma, the great soul of the universe.'

Ancient Buddhist temple at Bodh Gaya, India, restored in 1884.

A Tibetan prayer-wheel.

"After the world had appeared by the mere wish of Para-Brahma, God created men, whom he divided into four classes, according to their color: white (Brahmans), red (Kshatriyas) [Kshatriya], yellow (Vaisyas) [Vaishya], and black (Soudras) [Sudras]. Brahma drew the first [the white caste] from his own mouth, and gave them as their portion the government of the world, the teaching of the laws to men, and the power to heal and judge them. The Brahman alone, therefore, occupy the position of priests, and the preachers, or commentators of the Vedas only, must adopt celibacy.

"The second caste, the [red] Kshatriyas, came from the hand of Brahma. These he made warriors, intrusting them with the mission of defending and protecting society. The kings, princely rulers, governors, and troops, belong to this caste, which enjoys relations of the greatest cordiality with the Brahmans, because one can not exist without the other; and the peace of the country depends on the alliance of the sword and the light, of the temple of Brahma, and the royal throne.

"The [yellow] Vaisyas, who compose the third caste, were drawn by Brahma from his own entrails. They are destined to the plowing of the fields and the breeding of animals, to the exercise of all kinds of trades and commerce, that they may support the Brahmans and Kshatriyas. They are authorized to enter the temple and listen to the reading of the Vedas on feast days only, being obliged to remain at their business affairs on all other occasions.

A version of the Trimurti, or Hindu Holy Trinity.

"The lowest caste, the blacks or Soudras [Sudras], came from the feet of Brahma to be the humble servants and slaves of the three first castes. They are forbidden to attend the reading of the Vedas; and to come in contact with them means contamination. They are wretched beings, robbed of all human rights, not daring to even gaze at the members of the superior castes, or defend themselves, and, in case of sickness, deprived of the care of a physician.

"A brass image from Ceylon of Gautama Buddha seated on the Mucalinda Serpent in an attitude of profound meditation, with eyes half-closed, and five rays of light emerging from the crown of his head."

"Death alone can free them from the consequences of their life of servitude; but to obtain this reward they must, during their entire life, cheerfully and faithfully serve a member of one of the privileged classes. Then only, after having performed these functions with excessive zeal and fidelity in the service of a Brahman or a Kshatriya, can the Soudra entertain the hope that, after death, his soul shall be elevated to a superior caste.

"Should a Soudra be found wanting in respect toward a member of the privileged classes, or otherwise merit disgrace, he is expelled from his caste, degraded to the rank of a pariah, and banished from cities and villages; he becomes an object of universal contempt, considered as an abject creature, and permitted to perform only the basest and most menial labor.

"The same punishment may, it is true, be inflicted upon a member of any other caste; but by dint of repentance, of fastings and privations, the latter may in time regain their former rank, while the wretched Soudra is forever lost if once expelled from his caste.

"It is therefore easy to understand the veneration of the Vaisyas and the Soudras for Jesus, who, notwithstanding the threats of the Brahmans, never abandoned them.

"In his sermons, Jesus not only inveighed against the injustice of depriving a man of his right to be considered as such, while a monkey, or a piece of marble and metal was worshiped, but also denounced the main principle of Brahmanism, its system of gods, its doctrine, and its trimourti [Trimurti] (trinity), the keystone of this religion.

"Para-Brahma is represented with three faces on one single head: This is the trimourti (trinity), composed of Brahma (the creator), Vischnou [Vishnu] (the preserver), and Siva [Shiva] (the destroyer).

"The origin of the trimourti is as follows:

"In the beginning, Para-Brahma created the waters and cast upon them the generating seed, which was transformed into a dazzling egg reflecting the image of Brahma. Millions of centuries later, Brahma divided this egg into two parts, the upper half of which became heaven and the lower half the earth. This done, Brahma came down upon this earth in the appearance of a child, placed himself on a lotus flower, withdrew within himself and propounded this question: 'Who shall watch over the preservation of what I have created?' The answer came from his own mouth as flame: 'I,' and Brahma gave this word the name of Vischnou, which signifies, 'he who preserves.' Brahma then divided his being into two halves, one male and the other female, the active world and the passive world, the union of which brought forth Siva, 'the destroyer.'

"The attributes of the trimourti are: Brahma, the creator being; Vischnou, the preserving wisdom; Siva, the destructive wrath of justice. Brahma is the substance from which all things are made; Vischnou, the space in which everything lives; and Siva, time which destroys all things.

"Brahma is the face that animates everything; Vischnou, the water that sustains the strength of creatures; Siva, the fire that breaks the links that unite objects. Brahma is the past, Vischnou the present, and Siva the future. Each part of the trimourti, moreover, possesses a wife: That of Brahma is Sarasvati [Saraswati], goddess of wisdom; that of Vischnou is called Lackmi [Lakshmi], goddess of virtue; and Siva is married to Kali, goddess of death, the universal destroyer.

"From this last union was born the wise god, Ganega, and Indra, chief of the inferior divinities, the number of which, including all objects of adoration belonging to the Hindoos, comes to three hundred millions.

"Vischnou came down upon earth eight times, incarnating himself first in a fish, to save the sacred books from the deluge, then successively in a turtle, a dwarf, a wild boar, a lion, later in Rama—who was a king's son—in Krichna, and finally in Buddha. He will come a ninth time under the form of a cavalier mounted on a white horse, to destroy death and sin.

"Jesus denied the existence of all these hierarchal absurdities of gods which obscured the great principle of monotheism.

Lamieroo, Tibet.

An ancient Buddhist temple as it appeared in 1880. It was erected around 150 A.D. on the spot where Buddha is said to have attained satori (enlightenment).

"Seeing that the people were beginning to embrace the doctrines of Jesus, whom they had hoped to gain on their side, and who was now their adversary, the Brahmans resolved to assassinate him; but being warned in time by his devoted servants, he fled and took refuge in the mountains of Nepal.

"Buddhism had already taken deep root in this country at that period. This schism was remarkable for its moral principles and ideas on the nature of the divinity, which brought man and nature, and men among themselves, nearer together.

"The founder of the sect, Cakya-Mouni, was born fifteen hundred years before Christ at Kapila, the capital of his father's kingdom, near Nepal in the Himalayas. He belonged to the Gothamide race and to the ancient family of Cakyas. He evinced a strong attachment to religion from childhood, and, notwithstanding his father's objections and disapproval, left the palace in which he lived with all its luxuries. He immediately began to preach against the Brahmans, meanwhile purifying their doctrine. He died at Koucinagara [Kushinagar, India], surrounded by many of his faithful disciples. His body was burned, and his ashes distributed among the cities in which his new doctrine had replaced Brahmanism.

"According to the Buddhist doctrine, the Creator always remains in a state of absolute inaction which nothing can disturb, and from which he arouses only at certain epochs determined by fate, in order to create terrestrial Buddhas. To this end, the Spirit is detached from the sovereign Creator and incarnated in a Buddha, in whom it dwells for some time on earth, where it creates buddhissatwas [Bodhisattvas] (masters) whose mission it is to preach the divine word and found new churches of believers, to whom they shall give laws and for whom they will institute a new religious order according to the traditions of Buddhism.

"A terrestrial Buddha is, in some sort, a reflection of the sovereign Creator Buddha, to whom he again unites himself after the termination of his existence on earth; so it is with the Buddhissatwas who, as a reward for their works and the privations they have endured here below, receive eternal beatitude and enjoy a repose nothing can disturb.

"Jesus spent six years among the Buddhists, where he found the principle of monotheism still in its purity. Having attained the age of twenty-six years he bethought himself of his native country, which labored under a foreign yoke. He therefore resolved to return there. While journeying thither he continued to preach against idolatry, human sacrifices, and religious errors, exhorting the people to acknowledge and adore God, the father of all creatures whom he cherishes equally, the masters as well as the slaves, for they are all his children, to whom he has given his beautiful universe as a common inheritance. The sermons of Jesus often produced a deep impression upon the nations he visited, where he braved many dangers instigated by the priests, but was as often protected by the idolaters, who, only the day before, had sacrificed their children to the idols.

Polytheistic Hinduism has over 300 million deities, a fact that greatly displeased the monotheistic Jesus.

"While crossing Persia, Jesus almost caused an uprising among the followers of the doctrine of Zoroaster. Fearing the vengeance of the people, however, the priests dared not assassinate him, but had recourse to a ruse instead, and drove him from the town during the night, hoping he might be devoured by wild beasts. But Jesus escaped this peril and arrived safe and sound in the land of Israel.

"It must be here remarked that the Orientals, in the midst of their picturesque wretchedness and the ocean of depravity in which they have sunk, under the continued influence of their priests and preceptors, possess nevertheless a most pronounced predilection for instruction and readily understand properly applied explanations. More than once, by the aid of some simple words of truth, I have successfully appealed to the conscience of a thief or an unruly servant. These people, moved by a sentiment of innate honesty, which the clergy, to further their own personal ends, endeavor by all possible means to stifle—these people, I repeat, are very quick to learn the principles of honesty, and exhibit the greatest contempt for those who have abused them.

Jesus raising the daughter of Jairus from the dead.

"By virtue of a single word of truth, it is possible to make of all India, with its three hundred millions of idols [deities], a vast Christian country; but—this beautiful project would undoubtedly be prejudicial to certain Christians, who, like the aforesaid priests, speculate on the ignorance of the masses to enrich themselves.

"Saint Luke says that: 'Jesus was about thirty years of age when he began to exercise his ministry.' According to the Buddhist chronicler, Jesus would have commenced to preach in his twenty-ninth year. *All his sermons, which the Evangelists do not mention and which have been preserved by the Buddhists, are remarkable for their character of divine grandeur* [my emphasis, L.S.]. The fame of the new preacher spread rapidly through the country, and Jerusalem impatiently awaited his coming. When he drew near to the holy city, all the inhabitants went forth to meet him and conducted him in triumph to the temple, which is in conformity with the Christian tradition. The chiefs and the learned men who listened, admired his sermons and rejoiced at the beneficent impression produced on the multitude by the words of Jesus. All the remarkable sermons of Jesus are filled with sublime words.

"But Pilate, Governor of the country, did not see the matter in the same light. Zealous agents reported to him that Jesus announced the near approach of a new kingdom, the re-establishment of the throne of Israel, and that he called himself the Son of God, sent to revive the courage of Israel, for he, King of Judea, would soon ascend the throne of his ancestors.

"I have no wish to attribute to Jesus the role of revolutionist, but, to me, it seems very probable that he labored with the people with a view of re-establishing the throne that was his by right of inheritance. Divinely inspired, and at the same time fully convinced that his pretensions were legitimate, Jesus therefore preached the spiritual union of the people that a political union might result.

"Alarmed at these rumors, Pilate assembled the learned

men and the elders of the people, charging them to interdict Jesus from public preaching and condemn him in the temple under the accusation of apostasy. This was the easiest way of ridding himself of a dangerous man whose royal origin was known to Pilate, and whose fame was growing among the people.

Jesus being rejected by the Jews.

"It must be remarked on this subject, that far from persecuting Jesus, the Israelites, recognizing in him the descendant of the illustrious dynasty of David, made him the object of their secret hopes, as is proved by the scripture, which relates that Jesus preached openly in the temple in the presence of the elders, who had the power to prohibit him, not only access to the temple, but even of preaching in public.

"At Pilate's order, the Sanhedrim [Sanhedrin] assembled and cited Jesus to appear before its tribunal. At the conclusion of the inquest, the members of the Sanhedrim announced to Pilate that his suspicions were groundless, that Jesus was propagating religious truths, and not political ideas; that he preached the divine word, and that, furthermore, he claimed to have come, not to overthrow, but to re-establish the laws of Moses. The Buddhist chronicle only tends to confirm this sympathy which indubitably existed between Jesus, the young preacher, and the elders of the people of Israel; hence their response: 'We do not judge a just man.'

"Pilate was not reassured, however, and searched another opportunity of summoning Jesus before a regular tribunal; to this end, he sent many spies to watch him, and he was at length apprehended.

Jesus before Pilate.

Jesus being tormented by Roman soldiers as His followers
wail and lament.

"According to the Evangelists, it was the Pharisees and
the Hebrews who sought to put Jesus to death, while the
Buddhist chronicler positively declares that Pilate alone
must be held responsible. This version is evidently much
more likely than the account given by the Evangelists; the
conquerors of Judea being unable to long tolerate the
presence of a man who announced to the people their near
deliverance from the foreign yoke. The popularity of Jesus
having proved disquieting to Pilate, it was but natural that
he should dispatch spies with instructions to watch every
word and action of the young preacher. In their character
of inciting agents, these spies endeavored, by propounding
embarrassing questions to Jesus, to force him to utter some
imprudent words that might permit Pilate to proceed
against him. Had Jesus' preaching displeased the wise men

and Hebrew priests, they would simply have ordered the people not to listen to him or follow him, and have interdicted him entering the temple. The Evangelists, however, relate that Jesus enjoyed great freedom among the Israelites and in the temple, where Pharisees and learned men conversed with him.

"That he might succeed in condemning him, Pilate submitted him to inquisition, hoping to drive him to an avowal of high treason.

"Seeing that tortures did not bring about the desired result, and that, unlike other innocent persons put to the same suffering and agony, Jesus did not falter and accuse himself, Pilate commanded his servants to proceed to the utmost cruelty, that his death might be brought about by exhaustion: Jesus, however, finding a source of strength and courage in his own will and in his confidence in his cause, which was that of the nation and of God himself, opposed an unflinching endurance to all the refinements of cruelty received at the hands of his torturers.

"Jesus having undergone the secret inquisition, the elders were much displeased thereat; they therefore resolved to intercede in his favor and ask that he be set at liberty before the feast of the Passover.

"Foiled in the object of their demand by Pilate, they determined to insist upon having him brought before the tribunal, so certain were they of his acquittal, which seemed fully assured since the entire people ardently desired it.

"In the eyes of the priests, Jesus was a saint [Saint Jesus or Saint Issa] belonging to the house of David, and his unjust detention, or what was still more grave, his condemnation, would cast a deep gloom upon the solemnity of the great national feast of the Israelites.

"On learning of the refusal of their demand, they begged that the trial should take place before the feast. This time Pilate acceded to their wishes, but also ordered that two thieves should be tried at the same time. By this means Pilate strove to belittle, in the eyes of the people, the importance that might be attached to a judgment rendered against an innocent man if he were tried alone, thus leaving the nation under the sad impression of a verdict dictated beforehand; while, on the contrary, the simultaneous condemnation of Jesus and the two thieves would almost efface the injustice committed against one of the accused.

"The accusation was based upon the depositions of hired witnesses.

"During the trial, Pilate used the words of Jesus, who preached the Kingdom of Heaven [that is, the Gospel of the Kingdom of God],[132] to justify the accusation against him. He counted, it would seem, upon the effect produced by the replies of Jesus, as well as on his own personal authority to influence the members of the tribunal to not examine too minutely the details of the case before them to obtain the desired verdict.

Judas betrays Jesus.

Peter denying Jesus for the third time.

"After hearing the perfectly natural reply of the judges, that the words of Jesus only proved a sentiment diametrically opposed to the accusation, and that he could not be condemned thereon, Pilate had recourse to the only means left him, that is, to the deposition of an informer, who, in the Governor's judgment, could not fail to produce a deep impression on the judges. The wretch, who was none other than Judas [Iscariot], then formally accused Jesus of having incited the people to rebellion.

"Then [according to the Buddhist manuscripts, there] followed a scene of the grandest sublimity. While Judas gave utterance to his testimony, Jesus turned to him, and, having blessed him, said: 'Thou shalt be forgiven, for what thou sayest cometh not of thee.' Then turning to the Governor, he continued: 'Why lower thy dignity and teach thy inferiors to live in falsehood, since, even without this, thou hast the power to condemn an innocent man!'

"Touching and sublime words! Jesus Christ manifests himself in all his grandeur, first in showing the informer that he has sold his conscience, then in forgiving him; turning next to Pilate, he censured him for having recourse to proceedings so degrading to his dignity to obtain his condemnation.

"The accusation brought by Jesus against Pilate, caused the latter to completely forget his position and the prudence he should display; he therefore imperiously demanded the condemnation of Jesus at the hands of the judges, and, as if to assert the unlimited power he enjoyed, the acquittal of the two thieves.

"Finding this demand to discharge the two thieves and condemn Jesus, though innocent, too unjust to comply with, the judges refused to commit this double crime against their conscience and their laws; but being too weak to struggle against a man who had the power to give a final verdict, and seeing him determined to rid himself of a person who rivaled the Roman authorities, they left him to pronounce the judgment he so ardently desired. That they might not be censured by the people, who could not have forgiven so unjust a judgment, they washed their hands as they came out of the tribunal chamber, showing thereby that they were innocent of the death of Jesus, whom the multitude adored.

"About ten years ago I read an article on Judas in a German journal, the *Fremdenblatt*, in which the author endeavored to show that the informer had been Jesus' best friend. It would seem that it was through love for his master that Judas betrayed him, in his blind belief in the words of the Savior, who said that his kingdom would come after his crucifixion. But when he beheld him on the cross, after vainly awaiting his immediate resurrection, Judas found himself incapable of bearing his remorse and hanged himself.

"It is useless to elaborate on this lucubration, which is certainly original.

"But to return to the scriptural narrative and the

Buddhist chronicle, it seems quite probable that the hired informer may have been Judas, although the Buddhist version is silent on this point. As to the theory that remorse of conscience drove the informer to the taking of his own life, I place little credence in it. A man capable of committing an act of such cowardice and of bringing against any one of his fellow-men an accusation so notoriously false, and that, not from a spirit of envy or revenge, but for a mere handful of silver, such a man, I repeat, is psychologically worthless. He is ignorant of all idea of honesty or conscience, and remorse is unknown to him.

"It is to be presumed that the Governor took this matter into his own hands, as is sometimes done in our days, when it is imperative to keep from the people a grave and compromising secret which such a man might easily betray without heeding the consequences. Judas was no doubt hanged forthwith to prevent him from ever revealing that *the testimony on which Jesus was condemned emanated from the Governor himself* [my emphasis, L.S.].

Jesus is crucified between two thieves.

"On the day of the crucifixion, a large body of Roman soldiers was stationed about the cross to prevent the people from rescuing the object of their worship. In this circumstance, Pilate displayed extraordinary firmness and resolution. But though, owing to his precautions, an uprising was averted, he could not prevent the people from weeping over the downfall of their hopes, which died with the last descendant of the house of David. The entire population went to adore the tomb of Jesus, and though we have no precise details of the first days after the Passion, we may easily imagine the scenes that must have taken place. It is only reasonable to suppose that the prudent lieutenant of the Roman Cæsar, seeing that the tomb of Jesus was becoming a shrine of universal lamentations and the object of national mourning, and fearing that the memory of this just man might excite discontent and perhaps arouse the entire population against their foreign yoke, should have taken all possible means to divert the public mind from the recollection of Jesus. For three days, the soldiers placed on guard at the tomb were the butt of the jeers and maledictions of the people, who, braving the danger, came in throngs to adore the great martyr. Pilate therefore ordered his soldiers to remove the body during the night, when the pilgrimages had ceased, and inter it clandestinely in another place, leaving the first tomb open and unguarded, that the people might see that Jesus had disappeared.

"But Pilate failed to accomplish this end; for, on the following day, not finding the body of their master in the sepulcher, the Hebrews, who were very superstitious and believed in miracles, declared him resuscitated.

"How this legend came to be generally accepted, we know not. It may have existed for a long time in a latent state and been first spread among the lower classes; or, perhaps, the Hebrew ecclesiastics looked with indulgence upon this innocent belief which gave to the oppressed a shadow of revenge against their oppressors. However this may be, since the day this legend of the resurrection became known to all, no one has had the strength of mind to point out the impossibility of it.

"As concerns the resurrection itself, it must be remarked that, according to the Buddhists, the soul of the just man was united to the Eternal Being, while the Evangelists strongly insist upon the ascension of the body. It nevertheless seems to me, that the Evangelists and Apostles were wise in giving a plastic description of the resurrection; for otherwise, that is to say, had the miracle been less material, their sermons would not have been stamped, in the eyes of the people, with that divine authority, that character so manifestly divine which Christianity retains to this day, as being the only religion capable of maintaining the people in a state of sublime enthusiasm, of softening their savage instincts, and of bringing them nearer to the great and simple nature which God has confided, it is said, to the feeble dwarf called man."[133]

The empty tomb—not mentioned by Saint Paul, the founder of organized Christianity.

And here ends Notovitch's personal comments. In the following chapter I have included Notovitch's *complete* transcription of the original Buddhist text: *Life of Saint Issa, Best of the Sons of Men*. Afterward, I will close with my summation of our study.

The resurrected Jesus appearing to Mary Magdalene.

Chapter Five

THE ANCIENT CENTRAL ASIAN BOOK KNOWN AS
LIFE OF SAINT ISSA, BEST OF THE SONS OF MEN

The nearly 2,000 Year Old Buddhist Manuscript
recovered and published by Nicolas Notovitch

(ILLUSTRATIONS SELECTED & PLACED BY LOCHLAINN SEABROOK)

One

1. The earth has trembled and the heavens have wept, because of the great crime just committed in the land of Israel.

2. For they have put to torture and executed the great just Issa, in whom dwelt the spirit of the world.

3. Which was incarnated in a simple mortal, that men might be benefited and evil thoughts exterminated thereby.

4. And that it might bring back to a life of peace, of love, and happiness, man degraded by sin, and recall to him the only and indivisible Creator whose mercy is boundless and infinite.

5. This is what is related on this subject by the merchants who have come from Israel.

Two

1. The people of Israel, who inhabited a most fertile land, yielding two crops a year, and who possessed immense flocks, excited the wrath of God through their sins.

2. And he inflicted upon them a terrible punishment by taking away

their land, their flocks, and all they possessed; and Israel was reduced to slavery by the rich and powerful Pharaohs who then reigned in Egypt.

The nine pyramids of Giza as seen from the south.

3. The latter treated the Israelites more cruelly than animals, loading them with chains and putting them to the roughest labor; they covered their bodies with bruises and wounds, and denied them food and shelter,

4. That they might be kept in a state of continual terror and robbed of all semblance of humanity;

5. And in their dire distress, the children of Israel, remembering their heavenly protector, addressed their prayers to him and implored his assistance and mercy.

6. An illustrious Pharaoh then reigned in Egypt, who had become celebrated for his numerous victories, the great riches he had amassed, and the vast palaces which his slaves had erected with their own hands.

7. This Pharaoh had two sons, the younger of whom was called Mossa [Moses]; and the learned Israelites taught him divers sciences.

8. And Mossa was beloved throughout the land of Egypt for his goodness and the compassion he displayed for them that suffered.

9. Seeing that, notwithstanding the intolerable sufferings they endured, the Israelites refused to abandon their God to worship those created by the hands of man and which were the gods of the Egyptians.

Meremptah: Egyptian Pharaoh of the Exodus.

10. Mossa believed in their indivisible God, who did not allow their flagging strength to falter.

11. And the Israelite preceptors encouraged Mossa's ardor and had recourse to him, begging him to intercede with Pharaoh, his father, in favor of his co-religionists.

12. Prince Mossa pleaded with his father to soften the lot of these unhappy people, but Pharaoh became angry with him and only imposed more hardships upon his slaves.

13. It came to pass, not long after, that a great calamity fell upon Egypt; the plague decimated the young and the old, the strong and the sick; and Pharaoh believed he had incurred the wrath of his own gods against him;

14. But the prince Mossa declared to his father, that it was the God of his slaves who was interfering in favor of his unhappy people and punishing the Egyptians;

15. Pharaoh commanded Mossa, his son, to gather all the slaves of Jewish race, to lead them away to a great distance from the capital

and found another city, where he should remain with them.

16. Mossa announced to the Hebrew slaves that he had delivered them in the name of their God, the God of Israel; and he went with them out of the city and of the land of Egypt.

17. He therefore led them into the land they had lost through their many sins; he gave them laws and enjoined them to always pray to the invisible Creator whose goodness is infinite.

18. At the death of the prince Mossa, the Israelites rigorously observed his laws, and God recompensed them for the wrongs they had suffered in Egypt.

19. Their kingdom became the most powerful in all the world, their kings gained renown for their treasures, and a long period of peace prevailed among the children of Israel.

Moses receiving the Ten Commandments.

Three

1. The fame of the riches of Israel spread over all the world, and the neighboring nations envied them.

2. But the victorious arms of the Hebrews were directed by the Most High himself, and the pagans dared not attack them.

3. Unhappily as man does not always obey even his own will, the fidelity of the Israelites to their God was not of long duration.

4. They began by forgetting all the favors he had showered upon them, invoked his name on rare occasions only, and begged protection of magicians and wizards;

5. The kings and rulers substituted their own laws for those that Mossa had prepared; the temple of God and the practice of religion were abandoned, the nation gave itself up to pleasures and lost its original purity.

6. Many centuries had elapsed since their departure from Egypt, when God again resolved to punish them.

7. Strangers began to invade the land of Israel, devastating the fields, destroying the villages, and taking the inhabitants into captivity.

8. A throng of pagans came from over the sea, from the country of Romeles [Rome]; they subjected the Hebrews, and the commanders of the army governed them by authority of Cæsar.

9. The temples were destroyed, the people were forced to abandon their worship of the invisible God and to sacrifice victims to pagan idols.

10. Warriors were made of the nobles; the women were ravished from their husbands; the lower classes, reduced to slavery, were sent by thousands beyond the seas.

The Forum at Rome.

11. As to the children, all were put to the sword; soon, through all the land of Israel, nothing was heard but weeping and wailing.

12. In this dire distress the people remembered their powerful God; they implored his mercy and besought him to forgive them; our Father, in his inexhaustible goodness, heeded their prayers.

Four

1. And now the time had come, which the Supreme Judge, in his boundless clemency, had chosen to incarnate himself in a human being.

2. And the Eternal Spirit, which dwelt in a state of complete inertness and supreme beatitude, awakened and detached itself from the Eternal Being for an indefinite period,

3. In order to indicate, in assuming the human form, the means of identifying ourselves with the Divinity and of attaining eternal felicity.

4. And to teach us, by his example, how we may reach a state of

moral purity and separate the soul from its gross envelope, that it may attain the perfection necessary to enter the Kingdom of Heaven which is immutable and where eternal happiness reigns.

5. Soon after, a wonderful child was born in the land of Israel; God himself, through the mouth of this child, spoke of nothingness of the body and of the grandeur of the soul.

6. The parents of this new-born child were poor people, belonging by birth to a family of exalted piety, which disregarded its former worldly greatness to magnify the name of the Creator and thank him for the misfortunes with which he was pleased to try them.

7. To reward them for their perseverance in the path of truth, God blessed the first-born of this family; he chose him as his elect, and sent him forth to raise those that had fallen into evil, and to heal them that suffered.

The birth of Jesus—known as Saint Issa in Central Asia.

8. The divine child, to whom was given the name of Issa [Jesus], commenced even in his most tender years to speak of the one and indivisible God, exhorting the people that had strayed from the path of righteousness to repent and purify themselves of the sins they had committed.

9. People came from all parts to listen and marvel at the words of wisdom that fell from his infant lips; all the Israelites united in proclaiming that the Eternal Spirit dwelt within this child.

The teenage Jesus begins his journey toward India.

10. When Issa had attained the age of thirteen, when an Israelite should take a wife,

11. The house in which his parents dwelt and earned their livelihood in modest labor, became a meeting place for the rich and noble, who desired to gain for a son-in-law the young Issa, already celebrated for his edifying discourses in the name of the Almighty.

12. It was then that Issa clandestinely left his father's house, went out of Jerusalem, and, in company with some merchants, traveled toward Sindh [today a province of Pakistan]

13. That he might perfect himself in the divine word and study the laws of the great Buddhas.

Five

1. In the course of his fourteenth year, young Issa, blessed by God, journeyed beyond the Sindh and settled among the Aryas [Aryans] in the beloved country of God.

2. The fame of his name spread along the Northern Sindh [Pakistan]. When he passed through the country of the five rivers and the Radjipoutan [now part of northwestern India], the worshipers of the god Djaïne begged him to remain in their midst.

3. But he left the misguided admirers of Djaïne and visited Juggernaut, in the province of Orsis [modern Odisha, India, formerly Orissa], where the remains of Viassa-Krichnarest, and where he received a joyous welcome from the white priests of Brahma.

4. *They taught him to read and understand the Vedas, to heal by prayer, to teach and explain the Holy Scripture, to cast out evil spirits from the body of man and give him back human semblance* [my emphasis, L.S.].

5. He spent six years in Juggernaut, Rajagriha, Benares, and the other holy cities; all loved him, for Issa lived in peace with the Vaisyas [Vaishya] and the Soudras [Sudras], to whom he taught the Holy Scripture.

6. But the Brahmans and the Kshatriyas [Kshatriya] declared that the Great Para-Brahma forbade them to approach those whom he had created from his entrails and from his feet:

7. That the Vaisyas were authorized to listen only to the reading of the Vedas, and that never save on feast days.

8. That the Soudras were not only forbidden to attend the reading of the Vedas, but to gaze upon them even; for their condition was to perpetually serve and act as slaves to the Brahmans, the Kshatriyas, and even to the Vaisyas.

9. "Death alone can free them from servitude," said Para-Brahma. "Leave them, therefore, and worship with us the gods who will show their anger against you if you disobey them."

10. But Issa would not heed them; and going to the Soudras, preached against the Brahmans and the Kshatriyas.

Hari Parbat, a famous hill overlooking the city of Srinagar, India.

11. He strongly denounced the men who robbed their fellow-beings of their rights as men, saying: "God the Father establishes no difference between his children, who are all equally dear to him."

12. Issa denied the divine origin of the Vedas and the Pouranas [Puranas], declaring to his followers that one law had been given to men to guide them in their actions.

13. "Fear thy God, bow down the knee before Him only, and to Him only must thy offerings be made."

14. Issa denied the Trimourti [Trimurti, the pre-Christian Hindu Holy Trinity] and the incarnation of Para-Brahma in Vishnou [Vishnu], Siva [Shiva], and other gods, saying:

15. "The Eternal Judge, the Eternal Spirit, composes the one and indivisible soul of the universe, which alone creates, contains, and animates the whole."

16. "He alone has willed and created, he alone has existed from eternity and will exist without end; he has no equal neither in the heavens nor on this earth."

17. "The Great Creator shares his power with no one, still less with inanimate objects as you have been taught, for he alone possesses supreme power."

18. "He willed it, and the world appeared; by one divine thought, he united the waters and separated them from the dry portion of the globe. He is the cause of *the mysterious life of man* [my emphasis, L.S.], in whom he has breathed a part of his being."

The Hindu god Vishnu.

19. "And he has subordinated to man, the land, the waters, the animals, and all that he has created, and which he maintains in immutable order by fixing the duration of each."

20. "The wrath of God shall soon be let loose on man, for he has forgotten his Creator and filled his temples with abominations, and he adores a host of creatures which God has subordinated to him."

21. "For, to be pleasing to stones and metals, he [Man] sacrifices human beings in whom dwells a part of the spirit of the Most High."

22. "For he humiliates them that labor by the sweat of their brow to gain the favor of an idler who is seated at a sumptuously spread table."

23. "They that deprive their brothers of divine happiness shall themselves be deprived of it, and the Brahmans and the Kshatriyas shall become the Soudras of the Soudras with whom the Eternal

shall dwell eternally."

24. "For on the day of the Last Judgment, the Soudras and the Vaisyas shall be forgiven because of their ignorance, while God shall visit his wrath on them that have arrogated his rights."

25. The Vaisyas and the Soudras were struck with admiration, and demanded of Issa how they should pray to secure their happiness.

26. "Do not worship idols, for they do not hear you; do not listen to the Vedas, where the truth is perverted; do not believe yourself first in all things, and do not humiliate your neighbor."

27. "Help the poor, assist the weak, harm no one, do not covet what you have not and what you see in the possession of others."

Six

1. The white priests and the warriors becoming cognizant of the discourse addressed by Issa to the Soudras, resolved upon his death and sent their servants for this purpose in search of the young prophet.

2. But Issa, warned of this danger by the Soudras, fled in the night from Juggernaut, gained the mountains, and took refuge in the Gothamide Country, the birth-place of the great Buddha Cakya-Mouni, among the people who adored the only and sublime Brahma.

3. Having perfectly learned the Pali tongue, the just Issa applied himself to the study of the sacred rolls of Soutras [Sutras].

4. *Six years later, Issa, whom the Buddha had chosen to spread his holy word, could perfectly, explain the sacred rolls* [my emphasis, L.S.].

5. He then left Nepal and the Himalaya Mountains, descended into the valley of Rajipoutan and went westward, preaching to divers people of the supreme perfection of man,

6. And of the good we must do unto others, which is the surest means of quickly merging ourselves in the Eternal Spirit. "He who shall have recovered his primitive purity at death," said Issa, "shall have obtained the forgiveness of his sins, and shall have the right to contemplate the majestic figure of God."

7. In traversing the pagan territories, the divine Issa taught the people that the adoration of visible gods was contrary to the laws of nature.

8. "For man," said he, "has not been favored with the sight of the image of God nor the ability to construct a host of divinities resembling the Eternal."

9. "Furthermore, it is incompatible with the human conscience to think less of the grandeur of divine purity than of animals; or of works made by the hand of man from stone or metal."

Buddha at the moment of enlightenment.

10. "The Eternal Legislator is one; there is no God but him; he has shared the world with no one, neither has he confided his intentions to anyone."

11. "Just as a father may deal toward his children, so shall God judge men after death according to his merciful laws; never will he humiliate his child by causing his soul to emigrate, as in a purgatory, into the body of an animal" [known in Hinduism as the transmigration of souls].

12. "The heavenly law," said the Creator through the lips of Issa, "is

averse to the sacrifice of human victims to a statue or animal; for, I have sacrificed to man all the animals and everything the world contains."

13. "Everything has been sacrificed to man, who is directly and closely linked to Me, his Father; therefore, he that shall have robbed Me of My child shall be severely judged and punished according to the divine law."

14. "Man is as nothing before the Eternal Judge, to the same degree that the animal is before man."

15. "Therefore, I say to you, abandon your idols and perform no ceremonies that separate you from your Father and bind you to priests from whom the face of heaven is turned away."

16. "For it is they who have allured you from the true God, and whose superstitions and cruelty are leading you to perversion of the intellect and the loss of all moral sense."

Seven

1. The words of Issa spread among the pagans, in the countries through which he traveled, and the inhabitants abandoned their idols.

2. Seeing which, the priests demanded from him who glorified the name of the true God, proofs of the accusations he brought against them and demonstration of the worthlessness of idols in the presence of the people.

3. And Issa replied to them: "If your idols and your animals are mighty, and really possess a supernatural power, let them annihilate me on the spot!"

4. "Perform a miracle," retorted the priests, "and let thy God confound our own, if they are loathsome to him."

Jesus to His Disciples: "Follow me."

5. But Issa then said: "The miracles of our God began when the universe was created; they occur each day, each instant; whosoever does not see them is deprived of one of the most beautiful gifts of life."

6. "And it is not against pieces of in animate stone, metal, or wood, that the wrath of God shall find free vent, but it shall fall upon man, who, in order to be saved, should destroy all the idols they have raised."

7. "Just as a stone and a grain of sand, worthless in themselves to man, await with resignation the moment when he shall take and make them into something useful."

8. "So should man await the great favor to be granted him by God in honoring him with a decision."

9. "But woe be to you, adversary of man, if it be not a favor that you await, but rather the wrath of Divinity; woe be to you if you await until it attests its power through miracles!"

10. "For it is not the idols that shall be annihilated in His wrath, but those that have raised them; their hearts shall be the prey of everlasting fire, and their lacerated bodies shall serve as food for wild beasts."

11. "God shall drive away the contaminated ones of his flocks, but shall take back to himself those that have strayed because they misconceived the heavenly atom which dwelt in them."

12. Seeing the powerlessness of their priests, the pagans believed the words of Issa, and fearing the wrath of the Divinity, broke their idols into fragments; as to the priests, they fled to escape the vengeance of the people.

13. And Issa also taught the pagans not to strive to see the Eternal Spirit with their own eyes, but to endeavor to feel it in their hearts, and, by a truly pure soul, to make themselves worthy of its favors.

River footbridge leading to Kashmir.

14. "Not only must you desist from offering human sacrifices," said he, "but you must immolate no animal to which life has been given, for all things have been created for the benefit of man."

15. "Do not take what belongs to others, for it would be robbing your neighbor of the goods he has acquired by the sweat of his brow."

16. "Deceive no one, that you may not yourself be deceived; strive to justify yourself before the last judgment, for it will then be too late."

17. "Do not give yourself up to debauchery, for it is a violation of the laws of God."

18. "You shall attain supreme beatitude, not only by purifying yourself, but also by leading others into the path that shall permit them to regain primitive perfection."

Eight

1. The fame of Issa's sermons spread to the neighboring countries, and, when he reached Persia [Iran], the priests were terrified and forbade the inhabitants to listen to him.

2. But when they saw that all the villages welcomed him with joy, and eagerly listened to his preaching, they caused his arrest and brought him before the high-priest, where he was submitted to the following interrogatory:

3. "Who is this new God of whom thou speaketh? Dost thou not know, unhappy man that thou art, that Saint Zoroaster is the only just one admitted to the honor of receiving communications from the Supreme Being,

4. "Who has commanded the angels to draw up in writing the word of God, laws that were given to Zoroaster in paradise?"

5. "Who then art thou that darest to blaspheme our God and sow doubt in the hearts of believers?"

6. And Issa replied: "It is not of a new god that I speak, but of our heavenly Father, who existed before the beginning and will still be after the eternal end."

7. "It was of him I spoke to the people, who, even as an innocent

child, can not yet understand God by the mere strength of their intelligence and penetrate his spiritual and divine sublimity."

8. "But, as a new-born child recognizes the maternal breast even in obscurity, so your people, induced in error by your erroneous doctrines and religious ceremonies, have instinctively recognized their Father in the Father of whom I am the prophet."

9. "The Eternal Being says to your people through the intermediary of my mouth: 'You shall not adore the sun, for it is only a part of the world I have created for man.'"

A Buddhist votive-stupa at Bodh Gaya, India.

10. "'The sun rises that it may warm you during your labor; it sets that it may give you the hours of rest I have myself fixed.'"

11. "'It is to Me, and to Me only, that you owe all you possess, all that is around you, whether above or beneath you.'"

12. "But," interjected the priests, "how could a nation live according to the laws of justice, if it possessed no preceptors?"

13. Then Issa replied: "As long as the people had no priests, they were governed by the law of nature and retained their candor of soul."

14. "Their souls were in God, and to communicate with the Father, they had recourse to the intermediary of no idol or animal, nor to fire, as you practice here."

15. "You claim that we must worship the sun, the genius of Good

and that of Evil; well, your doctrine is an abomination, I say to you, the sun acts not spontaneously, but by the will of the Invisible Creator who has given it existence,

16. "And who has willed that this orb should light the day and warm the labor and the crops of man."

17. "The Eternal Spirit is the soul of all that is animated; you commit a grievous sin in dividing it into the spirit of Evil and the spirit of Good, for there is no God save that of good,

18. "Who, like the father of a family, does good only to his children, forgiving all their faults if they repent of them."

19. "And the spirit of Evil dwells on this earth, in the heart of men who turn the children of God from the right path."

Jesus lecturing the priests.

20. "Therefore I say to you, beware of the day of judgment, for God will inflict a terrible punishment on all who have turned his children from the right path and filled them with superstitions and prejudices,"

21. "On them that have blinded the seeing, transmitted contagion to the sound of health, and taught the adoration of things which God has subjected to man for his own good and to aid him in his labor."

22. "Your doctrine is therefore the fruit of your errors, for, in desiring to approach the God of Truth, you have created false gods."

23. After listening to him, the wise men resolved to do him no harm. In the night, while the city was wrapped in slumber, they conducted him outside the walls and left him on the highway, hoping that he might soon become the prey of wild beasts.

24. But, being protected by the Lord our God, Saint Issa continued his way unmolested.

Jesus is forced out of the city by angry Zoroastrian priests.

Nine

1. Issa, whom the Creator had chosen to recall the true God to the people that were plunged in depravities, was twenty-nine years of age when he arrived in the land of Israel.

2. Since the departure of Issa, the pagans [Romans] had heaped still more atrocious sufferings on the Israelites, and the latter were a prey to the deepest gloom.

3. Many among them had already begun to desert the laws of their God and those of Mossa [Moses], in the hope of softening their harsh conquerors.

4. In the presence of this situation, Issa exhorted his compatriots not to despair, because the day of the redemption of sins was near, and he confirmed their belief in the God of their fathers.

5. "Children, do not yield to despair," said the Heavenly Father through the mouth of Issa, "for I have heard your voices, and your cries have ascended to me."

6. "Weep not, O my beloved, for your sobs have touched the heart of your Father, and he has forgiven you as he forgave your ancestors."

7. "Do not abandon your families to plunge into debauchery, do not lose the nobility of your sentiments and worship idols that will remain deaf to your voices."

8. "Fill my temple with your hopes and your patience, and do not abjure the religion of your fathers, for I alone have guided them and heaped blessings upon them."

9. "Raise them that have fallen, feed them that are hungry, and help them that are sick, that you may all be pure and just on the day of the last judgment that I am preparing for you."

10. The Israelites flocked to hear the words of Issa, asking him where they should thank the Heavenly Father, since their enemies had razed their temples and laid violent hands on their sacred vessels.

11. Issa replied to them that God did not speak of temples built by the hands of men, but that he meant thereby the human heart, which is the true temple of God.

12. "Enter into your temple, into your own heart, illuminate it with good thoughts, patience, and the unflinching confidence you should place in your Father."

13. "And your sacred vessels are your hands and your eyes; look and do what is agreeable to God, for, in doing good to your neighbor, you perform a rite that embellishes the temple in which dwells the One who has given you life."

14. "For God has created you in his image; innocent, pure of soul, with a heart filled with kindness, and destined, not to the conception of evil projects, but to be the sanctuary of love and justice."

15. "Do not therefore sully your hearts, I say to you, for the Eternal Being dwells there always."

16. "If you wish to accomplish works stamped with love and piety, do them with an open heart, and let not your actions be inspired by the hope of gain or by thought of profit."

17. "For such deeds would not contribute to your salvation, and you would then fall into a state of moral degradation in which theft, falsehood, and murder, seem like generous actions."

"Jesus went from place to place strengthening, by the word of God, the courage of the Israelites."

Ten

1. Saint Issa went from place to place strengthening, by the word of God, the courage of the Israelites, who were ready to succumb under the weight of their despair, and thousands followed him to hear his preaching.

2. But the rulers of the cities feared him, and word was sent to the Governor, who resided in Jerusalem, that a man named Issa had come into the country, that his sermons excited the people against the authorities, that the crowd listened to him assiduously and neglected their duties to the State, claiming that soon they would be rid of their intruding rulers.

3. Then Pilate, the Governor of Jerusalem, ordered that the preacher Issa be arrested, brought to the city and conducted before the judges; not to arouse the dissatisfaction of the people, however, Pilate commanded the priests and the learned men, old men of Hebrew origin, to judge him in the temple.

4. Meanwhile, Issa, still continuing to preach, arrived in Jerusalem; having heard of his coming all the inhabitants, who already knew him by reputation, came to meet him.

5. They greeted him respectfully and threw open the doors of their temple that they might hear from his lips what he had said in the other cities of Israel.

6. And Issa said to them: "The human race is perishing because of its want of faith, for the gloom and the tempest have bewildered the human flock, and they have lost their shepherd."

7. "But tempests do not last forever, and the clouds will not hide the eternal light, the heavens shall soon be serene again, the celestial light shall spread throughout the world, and the strayed sheep shall gather around their shepherd."

8. "Do not strive to seek direct roads in the obscurity for fear of

stumbling into the ditch, but gather your remaining strength, sustain one another, place your entire trust in God, and wait till a streak of light appears."

Where ever Jesus went he argued with the religious hierarchy over their unspiritual doctrines.

9. "He that upholds his neighbor upholds himself, and whosoever protects his family protects his race and his country."

10. "For rest assured that the day of your deliverance from darkness is near; you shall gather together in one single family, and your enemy he who knows nothing of the favor of the Great God will tremble in fear."

11. The priests and the old men that listened to him, full of admiration at this language, asked of him if it were true that he had attempted to arouse the people against the authorities, of the country, as had been reported to the Governor Pilate.

12. "Is it possible to arise against misled men from whom the obscurity has hidden their path and their door?" returned Issa. "I have only warned these unfortunate people, as I warn them in this temple, that they may not advance further on their dark paths, for an abyss is yawning beneath their feet."

13. "Worldly power is not of long duration, and it is subject to innumerable changes. It would be of no use to a man to rebel against it, for one power always succeeds another power, and it shall be thus until the extinction of human existence."

14. "Do you not see, on the contrary, that the rich and the powerful are sowing among the children of Israel a spirit of rebellion against the eternal power of heaven?"

15. And the learned men then said: "Who art thou, and from what country hast thou come into our own? We had never heard of thee, and do not even know thy name."

16. "I am an Israelite," responded Issa, "and, on the very day of my birth, I saw the walls of Jerusalem, and I heard the weeping of my brothers reduced to slavery, and the moans of my sisters carried away by pagans into captivity."

17. "And my soul was painfully grieved when I saw that my brothers had forgotten the true God; while yet a child, I left my father's house to go among other nations."

18. "But hearing that my brothers were enduring still greater tortures, I returned to the land in which my parents dwelt, that I might recall to my brothers the faith of their ancestors, which teaches us patience in this world that we may obtain perfect and sublime happiness on High."

19. And the learned old men asked him this question: "It is claimed that you deny the laws of Mossa [Moses] and teach the people to desert the temple of God?"

20. And Issa said: "We can not demolish what has been given by our Heavenly Father and what has been destroyed by sinners; but I have recommended the purification of all stain from the heart, for that is the veritable temple of God."

21. "As to the laws of Mossa, I have striven to re-establish them in the heart of men; and I say to you, that you are in ignorance of their true meaning, for it is not vengeance, but forgiveness that they teach; but the sense of these laws have been perverted."

Eleven

1. Having heard Issa, the priests and learned men decided among themselves that they would not judge him, for he was doing no one harm, and having presented themselves before Pilate, made Governor of Jerusalem by the pagan king of the land of Romeles [Rome], they spoke to him thus:

2. "We have seen the man whom thou accuseth of inciting our people to rebellion, we have heard his preaching and know that he is of our people."

3. "But the rulers of the towns have sent thee false reports, for he is a just man who teaches the people the word of God. After interrogating him, we dismissed him that he might go in peace."

4. The Governor overcome with passion sent disguised servants to Issa, that they might watch all his actions and report to the authorities every word he addressed to the people.

Jesus was followed by multitudes of believers throughout His journeys.

5. Nevertheless Issa continued to visit the neighboring towns and preach the true ways of the Creator, exhorting the Hebrews to patience and promising them a speedy deliverance.

6. And during all this time, a multitude followed wherever he went, many never leaving him and acting as servants.

7. And Issa said to them: "Do not believe in miracles performed by the hands of man, for He who dominates nature is alone capable of

doing supernatural things, while man is powerless to soften the violence of the wind and bestow rain."

8. "Nevertheless, there is a miracle which it is possible for man to accomplish; it is when, full of a sincere faith, he resolves to tear from his heart all evil thought and, to attain his end, shuns the paths of iniquity."

9. "And all things which are done without God are but gross errors, seductions, and illusions, which only demonstrate to what point the soul of the man who practices this art is filled with deceit, falsehood, and impurity."

10. "Put no faith in oracles, God alone knows the future; he that has recourse to sorcerers defiles the temple within his heart and gives proof of distrust toward his Creator."

11. "Faith in sorcerers and their oracles destroys the innate simplicity and child-like purity in man; a diabolical power takes possession of him and forces him to commit all sorts of crimes and to adore idols."

12. "While the Lord our God, who has not his equal, is one, all-powerful, omniscient, and omnipresent; it is he who possesses all wisdom and all light."

13. "It is to him you must have recourse to be comforted in your sorrows, assisted in your toils, healed in your sickness; whosoever shall have recourse to him shall not be refused."

14. "The secret of nature is in the hands of God; for the world before appearing, existed in the depth of the divine mind; it became material and visible by the will of the Most High."

15. "When you wish to address him, become as children once more, for you know neither the past, nor the present, nor the future, and God is the master of time."

Twelve

1. "O just man," said the disguised servants of the [Pagan Roman] Governor of Jerusalem, "tell us should we do the will of our Cæsar or await our near deliverance?"

Jesus teaching the now suppressed and lost "Gospel of the Kingdom of God" (Mark 1:14).

2. And Issa, having recognized in his questioners the spies sent to watch him, said to them: "I have not said that you should be delivered from Cæsar; it is the soul plunged in error which shall have its deliverance."

3. "There can be no family without a head, and there would be no order in a nation without a Cæsar, who must be blindly obeyed, for he alone shall answer for his actions before the supreme tribunal."

4. "Does Cæsar possess a divine right," again questioned the spies, "and is he the best of mortals?"

5. "There is no perfection among men, but there are also some that are sick whom the men elected and intrusted with this mission must care for, by using the means that are conferred upon them by the sacred law of our Heavenly Father."

6. "Clemency and justice, these are the highest gifts granted to Cæsar; his name will be illustrious if he abides thereby."

7. "But he who acts otherwise, who goes beyond the limit of his power over his subject, even to placing his life in danger, offends the great Judge and lowers his dignity in the sight of men."

8. At this point, an aged woman, who had approached the group that she might better hear Issa, was pushed aside by one of the men in disguise who placed himself before her.

9. Issa then said: "It is not meet that a son should push aside his mother to occupy the first place which should be hers. Whosoever respecteth not his mother, the most sacred being next to God, is unworthy the name of son."

10. "Listen, therefore, to what I am about to say: Respect woman, for she is the mother of the universe and all the truth of divine creation dwells within her."

11. "She is the basis of all that is good and beautiful, as she is also the germ of life and death. On her depends the entire existence of man, for she is his moral and natural support in all his works."

12. "She gives you birth amid sufferings; by the sweat of her brow she watches over your growth, and until her death you cause her the most intense anguish. Bless her and adore her, for she is your only friend and support upon earth."

13. "Respect her, protect her; in doing this, you will win her love and her heart, and you will be pleasing to God; for this shall many of your sins be remitted."

14. "Therefore, love your wives and respect them, for to-morrow they shall be mothers, and later grandmothers of a whole nation."

15. "Be submissive toward your wife; her love ennobles man, softens his hardened heart, tames the beast and makes of it a lamb."

16. "The wife and the mother, inestimable treasures bestowed on you by God; they are the most beautiful ornaments of the universe,

and from them shall be born all that shall inhabit the world."

17. "Just as the God of armies separated day from night and the land from the waters, so woman possesses the divine talent of separating good intentions from evil thoughts in men."

18. "Therefore I say to you: After God, your best thoughts should belong to women and to wives; woman being to you the divine temple wherein you shall most easily obtain perfect happiness."

Women are a major theme in Jesus' unknown "Gospel of the Kingdom of God."

19. "Draw your moral strength from this temple; there you will forget your sorrows and failures, you will recover the wasted forces necessary to help your neighbor."

20. "Do not expose her to humiliation; you would thereby humiliate yourself and lose the sentiment of love, without which nothing exists here below."

21. "Protect your wife, that she may protect you and all your family; all that you shall do for your mother, your wife, for a widow, or another woman in distress, you shall have done for God."

Thirteen

1. Saint Issa thus taught the people of Israel for three years in every city, in every village, on the roadways, and in the fields, and all that he had predicted came to pass.

2. During all this time, the disguised servants of the Governor Pilate observed him closely, but without hearing anything that

resembled the reports hitherto sent by the rulers of the cities concerning Issa.

3. But the Governor Pilate, becoming alarmed at the too great popularity of Saint Issa, who, according to his enemies, wanted to incite the people and be made king, ordered one of his spies to accuse him.

4. Soldiers were then sent to arrest him, and he was cast into a dungeon where he was made to suffer various tortures that he might be forced to accuse himself, which would permit them to put him to death.

5. Thinking of the perfect beatitude of his brothers only, the saint endured these sufferings in the name of his Creator.

6. The servants of Pilate continued to torture him and reduced him to a state of extreme weakness; but God was with him and did not suffer him to die.

7. Hearing of the sufferings and tortures inflicted on their saint, the principal [Jewish] priests and learned elders begged the [Pagan] Governor to liberate Issa on the occasion of an approaching great feast.

8. But the Governor met them with a decided refusal. They then begged him to bring Issa before the tribunal of the Ancients, that he might be condemned or acquitted before the feast, to which Pilate consented.

9. On the morrow the Governor called together the chief rulers, priests, elders, and law-givers, with the object of making them pass judgment on Issa.

10. The saint was brought from his prison, and he was seated before the Governor between two thieves that were to be tried with him, to show the people that he was not the only one to be condemned.

11. And Pilate, addressing Issa, said: "O, man! is it true that thou hast incited the people to rebel against the authorities that thou mayest become king of Israel?"

12. "None can become king by his own will," replied Issa, "and they that have said that I incited the people have spoken falsely. I have never spoken but of the King of Heaven, whom I taught the people to adore."

Jesus before Pilate.

13. "For the sons of Israel have lost their original purity, and if they have not recourse to the true God, they shall be sacrificed and their temple shall fall in ruins."

14. "Temporal power maintains order in a country; I therefore taught them not to forget it; I said to them: 'Live in conformity to your position and fortune, that you may not disturb public order'; and I exhorted them also to remember that disorder reigned in their hearts and minds."

15. "Therefore the King of Heaven has punished them and suppressed their national kings; nevertheless, I said to them, if you resign yourself to your fate, the kingdom of heaven shall be reserved for you as a reward."

16. At this moment, witnesses were introduced; one of them testified as follows: "Thou hast said to the people that temporal

power was nothing to that of the King that shall free the Israelites from the pagan yoke."

17. "Blessed be thou," said Issa, "for having spoken the truth; the King of Heaven is more powerful and great than terrestrial laws, and his kingdom surpasses all the kingdoms here below."

18. "And the time is not far when, in conformity with the divine will, the people of Israel will purify themselves of their sins; for it is said that a precursor shall come to announce the deliverance of the nation and unite it in one family."

19. And addressing himself to the judges, the Governor said: "Hear you this? The Israelite Issa admits the crime of which he is accused. Judge him according to your laws and sentence him to capital punishment."

20. "We can not condemn him," replied the priests and the ancients; "thou hast thyself heard that he made allusion to the King of Heaven, and that he has preached nothing to the people which constitutes insubordination against the law."

21. The Governor then summoned [Judas] the witness who, at the instigation of his master, Pilate, had betrayed Issa; and when this man came he addressed Issa thus: "Didst thou not claim to be the king of Israel in saying that the Lord of heaven had sent thee to prepare his people?"

22. And Issa having blessed him, said: "Thou shalt be forgiven, for what thou sayest cometh not of thee!" Then turning to the Governor, he continued: "Why lower thy dignity and teach thy inferiors to live in falsehood, since, even without this, thou hast the power to condemn an innocent man!"

23. At these words, the Governor became violently enraged and ordered the death of Issa, while he discharged the two thieves.

24. The judges, having deliberated among themselves, said to

Jesus is condemned.

Pilate: "We will not take upon our heads the great sin of condemning an innocent man and of acquitting two thieves, a thing contrary to our laws."

25. "Do therefore as thou pleases." Having thus spoken, the priests and wise men went out and washed their hands in a sacred vessel, saying: "We are innocent of the death of a just man."

Fourteen

1. By order of the Governor, the soldiers seized upon Issa and the two thieves whom they conducted to the place of torture, where they nailed them to the crosses they had erected.

2. All that day, the bodies of Issa and of the two thieves remained suspended, dripping with blood, under the guard of soldiers; the people stood around about them, while the parents of the crucified men wept and prayed.

3. At sunset, the agony of Issa came to an end. He lost consciousness, and the soul of this just man detached itself from his body to become part of the Divinity.

4. Thus ended the terrestrial existence of the reflection of the Eternal Spirit, under the form of a man who had saved hardened sinners and endured so much suffering.

5. Pilate, however, becoming alarmed at his own actions, gave up the body of the holy man to his relations, who buried him near the place of his execution; the multitude then came to pray over his tomb and filled the air with weeping and wailing.

6. Three days later the Governor sent his soldiers to take up the body of Issa and bury it elsewhere, fearing a general uprising of the people.

7. The following day the sepulcher was found open and empty by the multitude; and the rumor immediately spread that the Supreme Judge had sent his angels to take away the mortal remains of the saint in whom dwelt on earth a part of the Divine Spirit.

8. When this report came to the ears of Pilate he fell into a rage and forbade everyone, under penalty of perpetual slavery, to ever utter the name of Issa and to pray to the Lord for him.

The triumph of Christianity: "Glory to God in the Highest" (Luke 2:14).

9. But the people continued to weep and praise their master aloud; therefore many were placed in captivity, subjected to torture, and put to death.

10. And the disciples of Saint Issa left the land of Israel and went in all directions among the pagans, telling them that they must abandon their gross errors, think of the salvation of their souls, and of the perfect felicity in store for men in the enlightened and immaterial world where, in repose and in all his purity, dwells the great Creator in perfect majesty.

11. The pagans, their kings and soldiers, listened to these preachers, abandoned their absurd beliefs, deserted their priests and their idols to sing the praises of the all-wise Creator of the universe, the King of kings, whose heart is filled with infinite mercy. [End of the ancient Buddhist manuscript.]

The Ascendency of the Christian Faith.

Chapter Six

SUMMATION: THE MYSTERY CONTINUES

WE HAVE COVERED THE ENTIRE story, in abbreviated form, of what I call "The Greatest Jesus Mystery of All Time." We may not have come any closer to scientifically proving where Jesus was between the ages of 12 and 30, but we have uncovered and examined a plethora of both biblical and extrabiblical evidence suggesting that He spent those 18 years in Central Asia, studying under a variety of Buddhist and Tibetan masters, and possibly others as well, in lands as far flung as Greece, Iran, and Egypt.

We have studied the life and work of Nicolas Notovitch, who became the first Westerner to bring to light the existence of Buddhist manuscripts chronicling the story of Jesus' youthful educational period in Asia. While many have attempted to discredit Notovitch and his acquisition of the ancient book, *Life of Saint Issa, Best of the Sons of Men*, it makes little difference whether or not the Russian explorer was a charlatan or not.

For one thing, one must take into consideration the many Pagan elements in Jesus' teachings. Where did these originate? Where did our Lord pick up the Buddhist and Hindu doctrines of reincarnation, chakras, karma, the Third Eye, the Divine Feminine, yoga, the Law of Attraction, Theosis, the Great I AM, and meditation, among a myriad of others that could be mentioned? And why do so many of His statements and teachings parallel, and in some cases even perfectly duplicate, those found in such pre-Christian Central Asian books as the Bhagavad Gita?

More importantly, there is the widespread Eastern belief that Jesus spent his young adulthood in India and Tibet, a belief, actually now more a tenet, that continues to pervade the Asian continent to this day, from, as I wrote in Chapter Two, Israel and Iraq to China and Mongolia—a region covering the entire Near, Middle, and Far

East, and containing over half the world's population.

So thoroughly suppressed in the West have been the actual facts of Jesus' missing 18 years, that we will probably never know the full truth. However, it is hoped that my little book will help keep alive the various traditions and theories related to this vital and perplexing topic. It is, after all, an important and fascinating enigma, one that, if it is ever solved, promises to forever alter our view of both Jesus and Christianity wherever one stands on the spectrum of our glorious Faith: conservative, liberal, or mystical.

The End

"And this gospel of the kingdom shall be preached in all the world for a witness unto all nations" (Matthew 24:14).

𝔑𝔬𝔱𝔢𝔰

1. See Hoffman, passim; G. A. Wells, passim.
2. Feldman and Hata, pp. 55-66.
3. See Luke 2:8.
4. For more on this important topic see my book, *Christmas Before Christianity: How the Birthday of the "Sun" Became the Birthday of the "Son."*
5. Seabrook, *Seabrook's Bible Dictionary of Traditional and Mystical Christian Doctrines*, s.v. "Krishna"; s.v. "Mithra"; s.v. "Nativity."
6. Inferred from Luke 2:7, 12.
7. Matthew 2:1-12.
8. See e.g., Isaiah 47:13-15.
9. See e.g., Luke 21:25.
10. See e.g., Genesis 1:14; Daniel 1:20, 2:10; Psalm 19:1–2; Job 9:9; Jeremiah 10:2; Amos 5:8.
11. Compare Matthew 1:1-7 with Luke 3:23-38.
12. Matthew 1:16.
13. Luke 3:23.
14. Matthew 2:1.
15. Luke 1:26-27.
16. See e.g., Salm, passim.
17. Luke 3:23; 4:22.
18. Matthew 1:18-25.
19. For more on these particular topics see Strauss, pp. 108-118.
20. Schweitzer, pp. 6-7.
21. Schweitzer, p. 13.
22. Seabrook, *Seabrook's Bible Dictionary of Traditional and Mystical Christian Doctrines*, pp. 15-16.
23. Seabrook, *Seabrook's Bible Dictionary of Traditional and Mystical Christian Doctrines*, s.v. "Gospel (The)."
24. Luke 2:41-52.
25. Schonfield, *The Passover Plot*, pp. 54-55; Strauss, *The Life of Jesus Critically Examined*, pp. 193-194.
26. Josephus, *Life of Flavius Josephus*, p. 7.
27. Josephus, *Antiquities*, Book 2, Chapter 9, Verse 6.
28. 1 Samuel 2:26.
29. Strauss, *The Life of Jesus Critically Examined*, p. 195.
30. Graves and Podro, p. 763; Schonfield, *The Passover Plot*, p. 170.
31. See Schleiermacher, *A Critical Essay on the Gospel of St. Luke*, pp. 21-52.
32. Seabrook, *Seabrook's Bible Dictionary of Traditional and Mystical Christian Doctrines*, s.v. "Silent Years (The)."
33. See Luke 3:23.
34. For those interested in film, screenwriting, and screenplays, see my book: *A Rebel Born: The Screenplay*.
35. The four Gospels are so muddled, contradictory, and confusing that objective Bible scholars long ago gave up trying to piece together any type of coherent story of "The Life of Jesus." For more on this topic, see my book *Seabrook's Bible Dictionary of Traditional and Mystical Christian Doctrines*, s.v. "Jesus"; s.v. "Gospel (The)." Also see Strauss, Schleirmacher, and Schweitzer.
36. See John L. McKenzie, *Dictionary of the Bible*, individual New Testament entries.
37. See Miller; Barnstone (*The Other Bible*; *The Restored New Testament*); Grant (*Jesus*); Hoeller; Lange; Luomanen; Myer; Pagels (*The Gnostic Gospels*).
38. See Barnstone, *The Other Bible*, passim.

39. See, e.g., my books *Seabrook's Bible Dictionary of Traditional and Mystical Christian Doctrines*, s.v. "Gospel of Thomas"; and also *Jesus and the Gospel of Q.*

40. Seabrook, *Seabrook's Bible Dictionary of Traditional and Mystical Christian Doctrines*, s.v. "Nativity."

41. Seabrook, *Seabrook's Bible Dictionary of Traditional and Mystical Christian Doctrines*, s.v. "Silent Years (The)."

42. Luke 1:80.

43. Yogananda, Vol. 1, pp. 85, 86; Jacolliot, pp. 103-108.

44. *The Business Philosopher*, Vol. 19, December 1922, No. 12, p. 81.

45. Notovitch, p. x (Preface).

46. Yogananda, Vol. 1, p. 81.

47. Roerich, *Heart of Asia*, pp. 22-23.

48. Roerich, *Heart of Asia*, pp. 29-30.

49. Roerich, *Heart of Asia*, pp. 38-39.

50. Roerich, *Heart of Asia*, p. 127.

51. Roerich, *Altai-Himalaya*, pp. 125-126.

52. *Vide infra*, p. 69.

53. Yogananda, Vol. 1, pp. 82-84.

54. *The Literary Digest International Book Review*, pp. 626-627.

55. Seabrook, *Seabrook's Bible Dictionary of Traditional and Mystical Christian Doctrines*, s.v. "Silent Years (The)"; Seabrook, *Jesus and the Law of Attraction*, p. 508.

56. Matthew 24:14.

57. Mark 13:10.

58. Luke 24:47.

59. John 9:5.

60. 1 Timothy 3:16.

61. Matthew 17:20.

62. Mark 11:24.

63. Seabrook, *Jesus and the Law of Attraction*, p. 64. This law was set down by ancient Jews even earlier. The Book of Proverbs 23:7 succinctly proclaims: "As a man thinketh in his heart, so is he."

64. Matthew 6:22-29.

65. Revelation 1:16.

66. Revelation 1:11.

67. See, e.g., Galatians 4:21–31.

68. For more on all of these topics see my book, *Seabrook's Bible Dictionary of Traditional and Mystical Christian Doctrines*, passim.

69. Matthew 11:11-15.

70. Matthew 16:13-14.

71. Matthew 17:10-13. The following passages concerning the birth of John the Baptist, from the Gospel of Luke, corroborate the previous seemingly reincarnation-related statements by Jesus: "But the angel said unto him, 'Fear not, Zacharias: for thy prayer is heard; and thy wife Elisabeth shall bear thee a son, and thou shalt call his name John. And thou shalt have joy and gladness; and many shall rejoice at his birth. For he shall be great in the sight of the Lord, and shall drink neither wine nor strong drink; and he shall be filled with the Holy Ghost, even from his mother's womb. And many of the children of Israel shall he turn to the Lord their God. And he shall go before him in the spirit and power of Elias [my emphasis, L.S.] to turn the hearts of the fathers to the children, and the disobedient to the wisdom of the just; to make ready a people prepared for the Lord.'" Luke 1:13-17. Also see John 1:21. Some, like Paramahansa Yogananda, believe that Jesus was Elisha in a former incarnation, in which lifetime He and Elijah, who would later incarnate as John the Baptist, formed a guru-student relationship, with Elijah-John being the teacher and Elisha-Jesus being the pupil. See Yogananda, Vol. 1, pp. 36-50. Also see my book, *Seabrook's Bible Dictionary of Traditional and Mystical Christian Doctrines*, s.v. "Elias"; s.v. "Elisha."

72. John 3:3-8.

73. John 8:56-58.

74. John 9:1-3.

75. John 10:9. See also Revelation 3:12.

76. John 14:1-3.

77. Matthew 11:28-30.

78. Matthew 6:6.

79. John 10:30-38.

80. Exodus 3:13-14.

81. John 17:21.

82. Seabrook, *Jesus and the Law of Attraction*, p. 34.

83. John 8:23.

84. John 6:35.

85. John 10:7. In Hinduism, this cosmic "door" is viewed as a spiritual portal through which trained yogis can leave and reenter their physical bodies at will. Thus Jesus, speaking as the Indwelling Christ, said: " I am the door: by me if any man enter in, he shall be saved, and shall go in and out, and find pasture." John 10:9.

86. John 10:11.

87. John 8:12.

88. Revelation 1:18.

89. John 13:13.

90. Matthew 11:29.

91. John 18:37.

92. John 14:6.

93. John 15:1.

94. Mark 14:61-62.

95. Matthew 22:36-40.

96. John 14:26.

97. Matthew 6:14-15.

98. Matthew 26:52. Paul was also aware of this pre-Christian Pagan law. See e.g., also Galatians 6:7.

99. Seabrook, *Seabrook's Bible Dictionary of Traditional and Mystical Christian Doctrines*, s.v. "Silent Years (The)."

100. Mark 4:12.

101. For more on the many connections between the names Chrishna and Christ, see my book *Seabrook's Bible Dictionary of Traditional and Mystical Christian Doctrines*, s.v. "Christ."

102. Seabrook, *Seabrook's Bible Dictionary of Traditional and Mystical Christian Doctrines*, s.v. "Silent Years (The)."

103. John 14:20.

104. Seabrook, *Seabrook's Bible Dictionary of Traditional and Mystical Christian Doctrines*, s.v. "Silent Years (The)."

105. John 6:47.

106. Seabrook, *Seabrook's Bible Dictionary of Traditional and Mystical Christian Doctrines*, s.v. "Silent Years (The)."

107. John 8:32.

108. Seabrook, *Seabrook's Bible Dictionary of Traditional and Mystical Christian Doctrines*, s.v. "Silent Years (The)."

109. Matthew 5:16.

110. Seabrook, *Seabrook's Bible Dictionary of Traditional and Mystical Christian Doctrines*, s.v. "Silent Years (The)."

111. Revelation 22:13.

112. Seabrook, *Seabrook's Bible Dictionary of Traditional and Mystical Christian Doctrines*, s.v. "Silent Years (The)."

113. John 7:38. For more on the topic of the Hindu origins of the Bible, Judaism, and Christianity, see Whitney, *Life and Teachings of Zoroaster*.

114. See e.g., Matthew 4:23; 9:35; 24:14; Mark 1:14.

115. Luke 17:21.

116. Mark 1:1. Note: This is the only passage in the entire Bible where the phrase "The Gospel of Jesus Christ" appears.

117. For more on this gargantuan Christian catastrophe see my book, *Seabrook's Bible Dictionary of Traditional and Mystical Christian Doctrines*, pp. 22-23, 60, 75-78; s.v. "Baptism"; s.v. "Ecclesia"; s.v. "Gnosis"; s.v. "Good News (The)"; s.v. "Gospel of Jesus Christ"; s.v. "Gospel of Q"; s.v. "Gospel of the Kingdom of God"; s.v. "I AM"; s.v. "Jesus"; s.v. "Kingdom of God"; s.v. "Myth of Christ"; s.v. "Seven Stars"; s.v. "Silent Years (The)"; s.v. "Teacher of Righteousness"; s.v. "Water"; Appendix B.

118. For more on the Great Catholic Bible Revision, see my book *Seabrook's Bible Dictionary of Traditional and Mystical Christian Doctrines*, Appendix B, pp. 405-446.

119. For more on Jesus' original unredacted sayings, see my book *Jesus and the Gospel of Q.*

120. Seabrook, *Seabrook's Bible Dictionary of Traditional and Mystical Christian Doctrines*, s.v. "Silent Years (The)."

121. Seabrook, *Seabrook's Bible Dictionary of Traditional and Mystical Christian Doctrines*, s.v. "Silent Years (The)."

122. Seabrook, *Seabrook's Bible Dictionary of Traditional and Mystical Christian Doctrines*, s.v. "Silent Years (The)."

123. Seabrook, *Seabrook's Bible Dictionary of Traditional and Mystical Christian Doctrines*, s.v. "Silent Years (The)."

124. Matthew 5:5.

125. Seabrook, *Seabrook's Bible Dictionary of Traditional and Mystical Christian Doctrines*, s.v. "Silent Years (The)."

126. Luke 6:24.

127. Seabrook, *Seabrook's Bible Dictionary of Traditional and Mystical Christian Doctrines*, s.v. "Silent Years (The)."

128. Seabrook, *Seabrook's Bible Dictionary of Traditional and Mystical Christian Doctrines*, s.v. "Silent Years (The)."

129. Seabrook, *Seabrook's Bible Dictionary of Traditional and Mystical Christian Doctrines*, s.v. "Silent Years (The)."

130. For a deeper investigation into these topics see my book, *Seabrook's Bible Dictionary of Traditional and Mystical Christian Doctrines*.

131. Exodus 20:6; Proverbs 3:19.

132. Matthew 4:23; 9:35; 24:14; Mark 1:14.

133. Notovitch, pp. 147-183.

𝕭ibliography
And Suggested Reading

Abbot, Walter M. (ed.). *The Documents of Vatican II.* New York, NY: Guild Press, 1966.

Albertson, Edward. *Understanding Zen for the Millions.* Los Angeles, CA: Sherbourne Press, 1970.

Alighieri, Dante. *The Banquet of Dante Alighieri* (Elizabeth Price Sayer, trans.,) London, UK: George Routledge and Sons, 1887.

Allen, John Romilly. *Early Christian Symbolism in Great Britain and Ireland Before the Thirteenth Century.* London, UK: Whiting and Co., 1887.

Allen, Paula Gunn. *The Sacred Hoop: Recovering the Feminine in American Indian Traditions.* Boston, MA: Beacon Press, 1986.

Alter, Robert. *The World of Biblical Literature.* New York, NY: Basic Books, 1992.

Altizer, Thomas J. J. *The Gospel of Christian Atheism.* Philadelphia, PA: Westminster Press, 1966.

Ambauen, Andrew Joseph. *The World's Symbolism, or Nature Voices and Other Voices.* Chicago, IL: J. S. Hyland and Co., 1916.

Ambrose, Saint. *The Letters of S. Ambrose, Bishop of Milan.* Oxford, UK: James Parker and Co., 1881.

Amery, Colin, and Brian Curran Jr. *The Lost World of Pompeii.* New York, NY: Getty Publications, 2002.

Anderson, Frederick (ed.). *A Pen Warmed-Up in Hell: Mark Twain in Protest.* New York, NY: Perennial Library, 1972.

Anderson, Hugh. *Jesus and Christian Origins.* Oxford, UK: Oxford University Press, 1964.

Anderson, J. N. D. *Christianity and Comparative Religion.* 1970. Downers Grove, IL: InterVarsity Press, 1974 ed.

Andrews, Ted. *The Occult Christ: Angelic Mysteries, Seasonal Rituals, and the Divine Feminine.* St. Paul, MN: Llewellyn, 1993.

Andrewes, Antony. *The Greeks.* 1967. New York, NY: W. W. Norton, 1978 ed.

Angus, Samuel. *The Mystery-Religions and Christianity.* New York, NY: Charles Scribner's Sons, 1925.

Ankerberg, John, and John Weldon. *Cult Watch: What You Need to Know About Spiritual Deception.* Eugene, OR: Harvest House, 1991.

Ardrey, Robert. *African Genesis.* 1961. New York, NY: Dell Publishing Co. (Laurel edition), 1972 ed.

———. *The Territorial Imperative.* 1966. New York, NY: Delta, 1968 ed.

Arieti, James A. *Philosophy in the Ancient World: An Introduction.* Lanham, MD: Rowman and Littlefield, 2005.

Armstrong, April Oursler. *What's Happening to the Catholic Church.* Garden City, NY: Echo Books, 1967.

Arnold, Edwin. *The Light of Asia; or, The Great Renunciation: Being the Life and Teaching of Gautama, Prince of India and Founder of Buddhism.* Boston, MA: Roberts Brothers, 1892.

Aron, Robert. *Jesus of Nazareth: The Hidden Years.* New York, NY: William Morrow and Co., 1962.

Arterburn, Stephen, and Jack Felton. *Toxic Faith: Understanding and Overcoming Religious Addiction.* Nashville, TN: Oliver-Nelson Books, 1991.

Ashe, Geoffrey. The *Virgin: Mary's Cult and the Re-emergence of the Goddess.* 1976. London, UK: Arkana, 1988 ed.

———. *Dawn Behind the Dawn: A Search for the Earthly Paradise.* New York, NY: Henry Holt, 1992.

Asimov, Isaac. *A Short History of Biology.* Garden City, NY: Natural History Press, 1964.

Astrov, Margot (ed.). *The Winged Serpent: An Anthology of American Indian Poetry.* 1946. Greenwich, CT: Fawcett, 1973 ed.

Atkins, Gaius Glenn, and Charles Samuel Braden. *Procession of the Gods.* 1930. New York, NY: Harper and Brothers Publishers, 1936 ed.

Attwater, Donald. *The Penguin Dictionary of Saints.* 1965. Harmondsworth, UK: Penguin, 1983 ed.

Augustine, Saint. *The Confessions of St. Augustine, Bishop of Hippo* (circa 400). (J. G. Pilkington, trans.). Edinburgh, Scotland: T. and T. Clark, 1886 ed.

Baba, Meher. *Life At Its Best.* 1957. New York, NY: E. P. Dutton, 1976 ed.

Baigent, Michael, and Richard Leigh. *The Dead Sea Scrolls Deception.* 1991. New York, NY: Touchstone, 1993 ed.

Baigent, Michael, Richard Leigh, and Henry Lincoln. *Holy Blood, Holy Grail.* 1982. New York, NY: Dell, 1983 ed.

———. *The Messianic Legacy.* New York, NY: Dell, 1986.

Bainton, Roland H. *Here I Stand: A Life of Martin Luther.* 1950. New York, NY: Mentor, 1962 ed.

———. *Behold the Christ.* 1970. New York, NY: Harper and Row, 1976 ed.

Baldwin, James Mark (ed.). *Dictionary of Philosophy and Psychology.* 3 vols. New York: Macmillan Co, 1905.

Balfour, Edward. *The Cyclopedia of India and of Eastern and Southern Asia, Commercial, Industrial, and Scientific.* 3 vols. London, UK: Bernard Quatrich, 1885.

Banton, Michael (ed.). *Anthropological Approaches to the Study of Religion.* 1966. London, UK: Tavistock Publications, 1973 ed.

Barbanell, Maurice. *This is Spiritualism.* 1959. New York, NY: Award Books, 1967 ed.

Baring, Anne, and Jules Cashford. *The Myth of the Goddess: Evolution of an Image.* 1991. Harmondsworth, UK: Arkana, 1993 ed.

Baring-Gould, William S. (ed.). *The Annotated Sherlock Holmes.* Avenel, NJ: Wings Books, 1992 ed.

Barlow, Henry Clark. *Essays on Symbolism.* London, UK: Williams and Norgate, 1866.

Barnouw, Victor. *An Introduction to Anthropology: Physical Anthropology and Archaeology.* Homewood, IL: Dorsey Press, 1971.

Barnstone, Willis (ed.). *The Other Bible.* New York, NY: Harper and Row, 1984.

———. *The Restored New Testament: A New Translation With Commentary, Including the Gnostic Gospels Thomas, Mary, and Judas.* 2002. New York, NY: W. W. Norton and Co., 2009 ed.

Barnstone, Willis, and Marvin Meyer (eds.). *The Gnostic Bible: Gnostic Texts of Mystical Wisdom From the Ancient and Medieval Worlds.* Boston, MA: New Seeds, 2006.

Barrett, C. K. *The New Testament Background: Selected Documents.* 1956. New York, NY: Harper and Row, 1961 ed.

Barrett, William (ed.). *Zen Buddhism: Selected Writings of D. T. Suzuki.* New York, NY: Doubleday, 1956.

Basalla, George. *The Evolution of Technology.* 1988. Cambridge, UK: Cambridge University Press, 1999 ed.

Basham, Don. *Can a Christian Have a Demon?* Monroeville, PA: Whitaker House, 1971.

Baumgartner, Anne S. *A Comprehensive Dictionary of the Gods: From Abaasy to Zvoruna.* Seacaucus, NJ: University Books, 1984.

Bauval, Robert, and Adrian Gilbert. *The Orion Mystery: Unlocking the Secrets of the Pyramids.* New York, NY: Crown, 1994.

Bede. *Historia Ecclesiastica Gentis Anglorum (A History of the English Church and People).* C.E. 731. Harmondsworth, UK: Penguin, 1974 ed.

Begg, Ean. *The Cult of the Black Virgin.* Harmondsworth, UK: Arkana, 1985.

Bell, Robert E. *Women of Classical Mythology: A Biographical Dictionary.* 1991. Oxford, England: Oxford University Press, 1993 ed.

Ben-Abba, Dov. *Hebrew-English, English-Hebrew Dictionary.* Nazareth, Israel: Massada-Press, 1977.

Bennett, D. M. *The Gods and Religions and Ancient and Modern Times.* 2 vols. New York, NY: Liberal and Scientific Publishing House, 1880, 1881.

Bennett, Jonathan. *Rationality.* 1964. London, UK: Routledge and Kegan Paul Ltd., 1971 ed.

Bently, Peter (ed.). *The Dictionary of World Myth.* New York, NY: Facts on File, 1995.

Berens, Lewis Henry. *The Digger Movement in the Days of the Commonwealth as Revealed in the Writings of Gerrard Winstanley, the Digger.* London, UK: Simpkin, Marshall, Hamilton, Kent, and Co.,

1906.

Bernstein, Morey. *The Search for Bridey Murphy*. 1956. New York, NY: Pocket Books, 1978 ed.

Berry, Thomas Sterling. *Christianity and Buddhism: A Comparison and Contrast*. London, UK: Society for Promoting Christian Knowledge, 1891.

Besant, Annie, and C. W. Leadbeater. *Man: Whence, How and Whither - A Record of Clairvoyant Investigation*. 1913. Madras, India: Theosophical Publishing House, 1971 ed.

Beston, Henry. *The Outermost House*. 1928. New York, NY: Holt, Rinehart and Winston, 1956 ed.

Bettelheim, Bruno. *The Uses of Enchantment: The Meaning and Importance of Fairy Tales*. New York, NY: Vintage, 1976.

Bhaktivedanta, A. C. (Swami Prabhupada). *The Science of Self Realization*. 1977. Los Angeles, CA: Bhaktivedanta Book Trust, 1983 ed.

Bidmead, Julye. *The Akitu Festival: Religious Continuity and Royal Legitimation in Mesopotamia*. 2002. Piscataway, NJ: Gorgias Press, 2004 ed.

Biedermann, Hans. *Dictionary of Symbolism: Cultural Icons and the Meanings Behind Them*. 1989. New York, NY: Facts on File, 1992 ed.

Bierce, Ambrose. *The Collected Works of Ambrose Bierce*. Vol. 7. New York, NY: Neal Publishing Co., 1911.

Bilde, Per. *The Originality of Jesus: A Critical Discussion and a Comparative Attempt*. Göttingen, Germany: Vandenhoeck and Ruprecht, 2013.

Blackman, Aylward M. *Gods, Priests and Men: Studies in the Religion of Pharaonic Egypt*. (Alan B. Lloyd, ed.) 1998. New York, NY: Routledge, 2011 ed.

Blackwelder, Boyce W. *Light From the Greek New Testament*. 1958. Anderson, IN: Warner Press, 1959 ed.

Blavatsky, Helena Petrovna. *Isis Unveiled: A Master-key to the Mysteries of Ancient and Modern Science and Theology*. 3 vols. 1877. New York, NY: J. W. Bouton, 1892 ed.

———. *The Secret Doctrine: The Synthesis of Science, Religion, and Philosophy*. 2 vols. London, UK: Theosophical Publishing Society, 1893.

Bloodworth, Venice. *Key To Yourself*. 1952. Marina del Rey, CA: DeVorss and Co., 1980 ed.

Bloom, Harold. *The American Religion: The Emergence of the Post-Christian Nation*. New York, NY: Touchstone, 1992.

Blunt, John Henry (ed.). *Dictionary of Doctrinal and Historical Theology*. London, UK: Rivingtons, 1872.

Bly, Robert. *Iron John: A Book About Men*. 1990. New York, NY: Vintage Books, 1992 ed.

Blyth, Reginald Horace. *Games Zen Masters Play*. New York, NY: Mentor, 1976.

Boardman, John, Jasper Griffin, and Oswyn Murray (eds.). *The Roman World*. 1986. Oxford, UK: Oxford University Press, 1988 ed.

Boates, Karen Scott (ed.). *The Goddess Within*. Philadelphia, PA: Running Press, 1990.

Boer, Harry R. *Above the Battle? The Bible and Its Critics*. 1975. Grand Rapids, MI: William B. Eerdmans, 1977 ed.

Böhme, Jakob. *Mysterium Magnum, or An Exposition of the First Book of Moses Called Genesis*. 1623. London, UK: Henry Blunden, 1656 English ed.

Bonhoeffer, Dietrich. *The Cost of Discipleship*. 1937. New York, NY: Macmillan, 1975 ed.

Bonwick, James. *Egyptian Belief and Modern Thought*. London, UK: C. Kegan Paul and Co., 1878.

Booty, John E. *The Church in History*. New York, NY: Seabury Press, 1979.

Borg, Victor Paul. *The Rough Guide to Malta and Gozo*. London, UK: Rough Guides, 2001.

Bowden, John. *Archaeology and the Bible*. Austin, TX: American Atheist Press, 1982.

Bower, Hamilton. *Diary of a Journey Across Tibet*. London, UK: Rivington, Percival and Co., 1894.

Brantl, George. *Catholicism*. New York, NY: Washington Square Press, 1962.

Breasted, James Henry. *A History of Egypt: From the Earliest Times to the Persian Conquest*. New York, NY: Charles Scribner's Sons, 1905.

Brennan, J. H. *Five Keys to Past Lives*. 1971. New York, NY: Samuel Weiser, 1975 ed.

Brewster, Earl H. *The Life of Gotama the Buddha*. Kegan Paul, Trench, Trübner and Co., 1926.

Briffault, Robert Stephen. *The Mothers: The Matriarchal Theory of Social Origins*. 1927. New York, NY: Macmillan, 1931 ed.

Briggs, Katherine. *The Vanishing People: Fairy Lore and Legends*. New York, NY: Pantheon Books, 1978.

Bright, Bill. *The Holy Spirit: The Key to Supernatural Living*. San Bernardino, CA: Campus Crusade for Christ International, 1980.

Brinkley, Dannion. *Saved by the Light: The True Story of a Man Who Died Twice and the Profound Revelations He Received*. New York, NY: Harper, 1995.

Bromiley, Geoffrey W. (ed.). *The International Standard Bible Encyclopedia*. 1915. Grand Rapids, MI: William B. Eerdmans Publishing, 1982 ed.

Brooke, Stopford Augustus. *Faith and Freedom*. Boston, MA: George H. Ellis, 1881.

Brooks, Phillips. *Visions and Tasks and Other Sermons*. New York, NY: E. P. Dutton, 1886.

———. *The Mystery of Iniquity and Other Sermons*. London, UK: Macmillan and Co., 1893.

Brown, Henry (ed.). *Justin Martyr's Dialogue With Trypho the Jew*. 1745. Cambridge, UK: George Bell, 1846 ed.

Brown, Robert. *Semitic Influence in Hellenic Mythology*. New York, NY: Arno, 1977.

Bruce, F. F. *The New Testament Documents: Are They Reliable?* 1943. Downers Grove, IL: InterVarsity Press, 1980 ed.

Brunner, Hellmut. *An Outline of Middle Egyptian Grammar*. Graz, Austria: Akademische Druck, 1979.

Bucke, Richard Maurice. *Cosmic Consciousness: A Study in the Evolution of the Human Mind*. 1901. Philadelphia, PA: Innes and Sons, 1905 ed.

Budapest, Zsuzsanna Emese. *The Holy Book of Women's Mysteries*. 2 vols. 1979. Oakland, CA: Susan B. Anthony Coven, 1982 ed.

Budge, Ernest Alfred Wallis. *Egyptian Magic*. London, UK: Kegan Paul, Trench, Trübner and Co., 1901.

———. *The Book of the Dead*. 3 vols. Chicago, IL: Open Court, 1901.

———. *The Gods of the Egyptians, or Studies in Egyptian Mythology*. 2 vols. London, UK: Methuen and Co., 1904.

———. *The Egyptian Heaven and Hell* ("Books on Egypt and Chaldaea" series). London, UK: Kegan Paul, Trench, Trübner and Co., 1905.

———. *Egyptian Ideas of the Future Life*. ("Books on Egypt and Chaldaea" series, Vol. 3). London, UK: Kegan Paul, Trench, Trübner and Co., 1908.

———. *Osiris and the Egyptian Resurrection*. 2 vols. London, UK: Philip Lee Warner, 1911.

———. *Amulets and Talismans*. N.d. New York, NY: Citadel Press, 1992 ed.

Bulfinch, Thomas. *Bulfinch's Mythology*. 1855-1863. New York, NY: Modern Library, n.d.

Bullough, Sebastian. *The Church in the New Testament*. Westminster, MD: Newman Press, 1957.

Bullough, Vern L., and Bonnie Bullough. *The Subordinate Sex: A History of Attitudes Toward Women*. 1973. Baltimore, MD: Penguin, 1974 ed.

———. *Women and Prostitution: A Social History*. 1978. Buffalo, NY: Prometheus Books, 1987 ed.

Bultmann, Rudolf. *New Testament and Mythology and Other Basic Writings*. (Schubert M. Ogden, ed. and trans.) Philadelphia, PA: Fortress Press, 1984.

Bunsen, Christian Charles Josias. *Hippolytus and His Age; or, The Beginnings and Prospects of Christianity*. 3 vols. London, UK: Longman, Brown, Green, and Longmans, 1854.

Burke, James. *Connections*. Boston: Little, Brown and Co., 1978.

Burkitt, Francis Crawford. *Early Eastern Christianity: St. Margaret's Lectures, 1904, on the Syriac-Speaking Church*. New York, NY: E. P. Dutton, and Co., 1904.

Burnett, Frances Hodgson. *The Secret Garden*. 1911. New York, NY: Dell, 1974 ed.

Burr, William Henry. *Revelations of Antichrist, Concerning Christ and Christianity*. Boston, MA: J. P. Mendum, 1879.

Burrell, David James. *The Religions of the World: An Outline of the Great Religious Systems*. Philadelphia, PA: Presbyterian Board of Publication and Sabbath-School Work, 1888.

Burrell, Sidney A. *Handbook of Western Civilization: Beginnings to 1700* (Vol. 1). 1965. New York, NY: John Wiley and Sons, 1972 ed.

Burrows, Millar. *The Dead Sea Scrolls*. 1955. New York, NY: Viking Press, 1961 ed.

Burtt, Edwin A (ed.). *The Teachings of the Compassionate Buddha*. New York, NY: Mentor, 1955.

Busenbark, Ernest. *Symbols, Sex, and the Stars, in Popular Beliefs: An Outline of the Origins of Moon and Sun Worship, Astrology, Sex Symbolism, Mystic Meaning of Numbers, the Cabals, and Many Popular Customs, Myths, Superstitions and Religious Beliefs*. New York, NY: Truth Seeker Co., 1949.

Bushnell, Horace. *Nature and the Supernatural, as Together Constituting the One System of God*.

Edinburgh, Scotland: Alexander Strahan and Co., 1862.

Butler, Trent C. (ed.). *Holman Bible Dictionary*. Nashville, TN: Holman, 1991.

Cabot, James Elliot. *A Memoir of Ralph Waldo Emerson*. 2 vols. Boston, MA: Houghton, Mifflin and Co., 1887.

Caddy, Eileen. *The Spirit of Findhorn*. 1976. San Francisco, CA: Harper and Row, 1979 ed.

Caesar, Gaius Julius. *The Conquest of Gaul*. 52 B.C.E. Harmondsworth, UK: Penquin, 1951.

Calasso, Roberto. *The Marriage of Cadmus and Harmony* (Tim Parks, trans.). New York, NY: Knopf, 1993.

Calvocoressi, Peter. *Who's Who in the Bible*. 1987. Harmondsworth, UK: Penguin, 1990 ed.

Campanelli, Pauline. *Ancient Ways: Reclaiming Pagan Traditions*. 1991. St. Paul, MN: Llewellyn Publications, 1992 ed.

Campbell, Joseph. *The Hero With a Thousand Faces*. 1949. New York, NY: Bollingen Foundation, 1973 ed.

———. *The Masks of the Gods: Primitive Mythology*. Vol. 1. 1959. Harmondsworth, UK: Arkana, 1991 ed.

———. *The Masks of the Gods: Oriental Mythology*. Vol. 2. 1962. Harmondsworth, UK: Arkana, 1991 ed.

———. *The Masks of the Gods: Occidental Mythology*. Vol. 3. 1964. Harmondsworth, UK: Arkana, 1991 ed.

———. *The Masks of the Gods: Creative Mythology*. Vol. 4. 1968. Harmondsworth, UK: Arkana, 1991 ed.

———. *Myths to Live By*. New York, NY: Bantam, 1972.

———. *Transformations of Myth Through Time*. New York, NY: Harper and Row, 1990.

———. *The Power of Myth* (with Bill Moyers). New York, NY: Doubleday, 1988.

Campbell, Reginald John. *The New Theology*. New York, NY: Macmillan, 1908.

Camphausen, Rufus C. *The Encyclopedia of Erotic Wisdom*. Rochester, VT: Inner Traditions International, 1991.

Cantor, Norman F. *Inventing the Middle Ages*. New York, NY: William Morrow and Co., 1991.

Capra, Fritjof. *The Tao of Physics: An Exploration of the Parallels Bewteen Modern Physics and Eastern Mysticism*. 1975. Boston: Shambala Publications, 1991 ed.

Carey, George Washington, and Inez Eudora Perry. *God-Man: The Word Made Flesh*. Los Angeles, CA: Chemistry of Life, 1920.

Carlyle, Thomas. *Heroes, Hero-worship, and the Heroic in History*. New York, NY: Charles Scribner's Sons, 1841.

Carlyon, Richard. *A Guide to the Gods: An Essential Guide to World Mythology*. New York, NY: Quill, 1981.

Carpenter, Edward. *Pagan and Christian Creeds: Their Origin and Meaning*. New York, NY: Harcourt, Brace and Co., 1921.

Carson, Anne. *Goddesses and Wise Women: The Literature of Feminist Spirituality, An Annotated Bibliography*. Freedom, CA: The Crossing Press, 1992.

Carson, D. A. *The King James Version Debate: A Plea for Realism*. Grand Rapids, MI: Baker Book House, 1979.

Carter, Howard, and A. C. Mace. *The Discovery of the Tomb of Tutankhamen*. 1923. New York, NY: Dover, 1977 ed.

Carter, Mary Ellen. *Edgar Cayce on Prophecy*. New York, NY: Paperback Library, 1968.

Carus, Paul. *The Gospel of Buddha According to Old Records*. 1894. Chicago, IL: Open Court, 1895 ed.

———. *The History of the Devil and the Idea of Evil From the Earliest Times to the Present Day*. Chicago, IL: Open Court Publishing Co., 1900.

———. (ed.). *The Monist: A Quarterly Magazine Devoted to the Philosophy of Science*. Vol. 25. Chicago, IL: Open Court Publishing Co., 1915.

Case, Shirley Jackson. *The Historicity of Jesus*. Chicago, IL: University of Chicago Press, 1912.

Cashford, Jules. *The Moon: Myth and Image*. New York, NY: Four Walls Eight Windows, 2003.

Cassius, Dio. *The Roman History: The Reign of Augustus* (Ian Scott-Kilvert, trans.). C. 214-226. Harmondsworth, UK: Penguin, 1988.

Castaneda, Carlos. *A Separate Reality: Further Conversations with Don Juan*. 1971. New York, NY:

Pocket Books, 1974 ed.

Cavalli-Sforza, Luigi Luca, and Francesco Cavalli-Sforza. *The Great Human Diasporas: The History of Diversity and Evolution.* 1993. Reading, MA: Helix Books, 1995 ed.

Cavendish, Richard. *A History of Magic.* 1987. Harmondsworth, UK: Arkana, 1990 ed.

Celeste. *The Messianic Legacy in the Age of Aquarius: Jesus, Redeemer of the World's Soul.* Bloomington, IN: AuthorHouse, 2007.

Cerminara, Gina. *Many Mansions.* 1950. New York, NY: Signet, 1967 ed.

——. *Many Lives, Many Loves.* 1963. New York, NY: Signet, 1974 ed.

Chadwick, Owen. *The Reformation.* 1964. Harmondsworth, UK: Penguin, 1976 ed.

Chaisson, Eric. *Cosmic Dawn.* New York, NY: Berkley Books, 1984.

Channing, William Ellery. *The Complete Works of W. E. Channing.* London, UK: Williams and Norgate, 1880.

Chapman, Graham, John Cleese, Terry Gilliam, Eric Idle, Terry Jones, and Michael Palin. *Monty Python's The Meaning of Life.* New York, NY: Grove Press, 1983.

Charig, Alan. *A New Look at the Dinosaurs.* London, UK: Heinemann Ltd. (published in association with the British Museum of Natural History), 1983 ed.

Chase, Mary Ellen. *The Bible and the Common Reader.* 1944. New York, NY: Macmillan, 1968 ed.

Chatterjee, Ramananda (ed.). *The Modern Review: A Monthly Review and Miscellany* (Vol. 9, January to June 1911). West Bengal, India: Prabasi Press, 1911.

Chernin, Kim. *Reinventing Eve: Modern Woman in Search of Herself.* 1987. New York, NY: Harper Collins, 1994 ed.

Chetwynd, Tom. *Dictionary of Sacred Myth.* London, UK: Aquarian Press, 1986.

Christian, C. W. *Friedrich Schleiermacher.* (From the book series: "Makers of the Modern Theological Mind.") Peabody, MA: Hendrickson, 1991.

Christie-Murray, David. *A History of Heresy.* Oxford, UK: Oxford University Press, 1976.

Chronicle of the World. Mount Kisco, NY: Ecam Publications, 1989.

Church History in the Fulness of Times. Church Educational System (eds.). Salt Lake City, UT: The Church of Jesus Christ of Latter-Day Saints, 1989.

Cirlot, J. E. *A Dictionary of Symbols.* 1962. New York, NY: Philosophical Library, 1983 ed.

Clark, Jerome. *Unexplained: 347 Strange Sightings, Incredible Occurrences, and Puzzling Physical Phenomena.* Detroit, MI: Visible Ink Press, 1993.

Clark, W. E. Le Gros. *History of the Primates.* 1949. Chicago, IL: University of Chicago Press, 1968 ed.

——. *The Antecedents of Man.* 1959. New York, NY: Quadrangle Books, 1978 ed.

Clarke, James Freeman. *Ten Great Religions: An Essay in Comparative Theology.* Boston, MA: Houghton, Mifflin and Co., 1871.

Clarke, O. Fielding. *For Christ's Sake.* New York, NY: Morehouse-Barlow, 1963.

Clymer, Reuben Swinburne. *The Rosicrucians: Their Teachings and Mysteries According to the Manifestoes Issued at Various Times by the Fraternity Itself.* 1903. Allentown, PA: Philosophical Publishing Co., 1910 ed.

Coates, James. *In Mormon Circles: Gentiles, Jack Mormons, and Latter-Day Saints.* 1990. Reading, MA: Addison-Wesley, 1992 ed.

Cohen, Daniel. *The Encyclopedia of the Strange.* New York, NY: Avon Books, 1985.

Cohen, Edmund. *The Mind of the Bible-Believer.* 1986. Buffalo, NY: Prometheus Books, 1988 ed.

Cole, Henry Hardy. *Illustrations of Ancient Buildings in Kashmir.* London, UK: India Museum, William H. Allen, 1869.

Coleman, Richard J. *Issues of Theological Conflict: Evangelicals and Liberals.* 1972. Grand Rapids, MI: William B. Eerdmans, 1980 ed.

Collignon, Maxime. *Manual of Mythology, in Relation to Greek Art* (Jane E. Harrison, trans.). London, UK: H. Grevel and Co., 1890.

Collins, Sheila D. *A Different Heaven and Earth.* Valley Forge, PA: Judson Press, 1974.

Comay, Joan. *Who's Who in the Old Testament.* 1971. New York, NY: Oxford University Press, 1993 ed.

Combes, Abbé (ed.). *Collected Poems of Saint Thérèse of Lisieux.* New York, NY: Sheed and Ward, 1949.

Compton's Encyclopedia and Fact-Index. 1922. Chicago, IL: F. E. Compton Co., 1969 ed.

Compton's Pictured Encyclopedia. 1922. Chicago, IL: F. E. Compton Co., 1957 ed.

Comte, Auguste. *Catéchisme Positiviste.* Paris, France: Ernest Leroux, 1874.

Conaty, Thomas James. *New Testament Studies: The Principal Events in the Life of Our Lord.* New York, NY: Benziger Brothers, 1898.

Condon, R. J. *Our Pagan Christmas.* Austin, TX: American Atheist Press, 1989.

Conway, J. D. *What the Church Teaches.* New York, NY: Harper and Brothers, 1962.

Coogan, Michael D. (ed.). *The Oxford History of the Biblical World.* Oxford, UK: Oxford University Press, 1998.

Cooper, J. C. *Symbolic and Mythological Animals.* London, UK: Aquarian Press, 1992.

Cooper-Oakley, Isabel. *Mystical Traditions.* Milan, Italy: Ars Regia, 1909.

Cooper, William Ricketts. *The Horus Myth in its Relation to Christianity.* London, UK: Hardwicke and Bogue, 1877.

Copan, Paul, and Kenneth D. Litwack. *The Gospel in the Marketplace of Ideas: Paul's Mars Hill Experience for Our Pluralistic World.* Downers Grove, IL: InterVarsity Press, 2014.

Corban, Jean. *Path to Freedom: Christian Experiences and the Bible.* New York, NY: Sheed and Ward, 1969.

Cotterell, Arthur. *A Dictionary of World Mythology.* 1979. New York, NY: Oxford University Press, 1990 ed.

———. *The Macmillan Illustrated Encyclopedia of Myths and Legends.* New York, NY: Macmillan, 1989.

Courtenay, William J. *The Judeo-Christian Heritage.* New York, NY: Holt, Rinehart and Winston, 1970.

Courtney, W. L. *The Literary Man's Bible.* London, UK: Chapman and Hall, 1908.

Cousteau, Jacques-Yves, and the staff of the Cousteau Society. *The Cousteau Almanac.* Garden City, NY: Doubleday, 1980.

Covell, Ralph. *Confucius, the Buddha, and Christ: A History of the Gospel in Chinese.* 1986. Eugene, OR: Wipf and Stock, 2004 ed.

Cover, Lois Brauer. *Anthropology For Our Times.* New York, NY: Oxford Book Co., 1971.

Cox, George W. *The Mythology of the Aryan Nations.* 2 vols. London, UK: Longmans, Green and Co., 1870.

Cramer, Raymond L. *The Psychology of Jesus and Mental Health.* 1959. Grand Rapids, MI: Zondervan, 1972 ed.

Cranston, Ruth. *The Miracle of Lourdes.* New York, NY: Popular Library, 1955.

Crisp, Oliver D. *God Incarnate: Explorations in Christology.* London, UK: T. and T. Clark, 2009.

Cross, Frank Leslie, and Elizabeth Anne Livingstone (eds.). *The Oxford Dictionary of the Christian Church.* 1957. London, UK: Oxford University Press, 1974 ed.

Crossley, Fred H. *English Church Design, 1040-1540 A.D.* 1945. London, UK: B. T. Batson, 1948 ed.

Cumont, Franz. *The Mysteries of Mithra.* London, UK: Kegan Paul, Trench, Trübner and Co., 1903.

———. *The Oriental Religions in Roman Paganism.* Chicago, IL: Open Court, 1911.

Curran, Charles E. *Transition and Tradition in Moral Theology.* Notre Dame, IN: University of Notre Dame Press, 1979.

Curtiss, Harriette Augusta, and F. Homer Curtiss. *The Key to the Universe, or a Spiritual Interpretation of Numbers and Symbols.* Washington, DC: The Curtiss Philosophic Book Co., 1917.

———. *The Key of Destiny: A Sequel to the Key of the Universe.* New York, NY: E. P. Dutton and Co., 1919.

Cushing, Josiah Nelson. *Christ and Buddha.* Philadelphia, PA: American Baptist Publication Society, 1907.

Daly, Mary. *Beyond God the Father.* Boston, MA: Beacon Press, 1973.

———. *Gyn/ecology: The Metaethics of Radical Feminism.* Boston, MA: Beacon Press, 1978.

Daniel, Alma, Timothy Wyllie, and Andrew Rammer. *Ask Your Angels.* New York, NY: Ballantine, 1992.

Dante, Alighieri. *Inferno* (Thomas G. Bergin, trans.). New York, NY: Appleton-Century, 1948.

Daraul, Arkon. *A History of Secret Societies.* 1962. New York, NY: Pocket Books, 1969 ed.

Dart, John. *The Jesus of Heresy and History: The Discovery and Meaning of the Nag Hammadi Gnostic Library.* New York, NY: Harper Collins, 1988.

Das, Sarat Chandra. *Journey to Lhasa and Central Tibet*. London, UK: John Murray, 1904.

Dasgupta, Amitava, with Lochlainn Seabrook. *Autobiography of a Non-Yogi: A Scientist's Journey From Hinduism to Christianity*. Franklin, TN: Sea Raven Press, 2015.

Das, Lama Surya. *Awakening the Buddha Within: Eight Steps to Enlightenment*. New York, NY: Broadway, 1998.

Dass, Baba Hari. *The Yellow Book: The Sayings of Bab Hari Dass*. San Cristobal, NM: Lama Foundation, 1973.

Dass, Ram. *The Only Dance There Is*. Garden City, NY: Anchor, 1974.

Daton, Lois. *Lilith*. Indianapolis, IN: Rod's Composing Service, 1977.

David, Bruno, Bryce Barker, and Ian J. McNiven (eds.). *The Social Archaeology of Australian Indigenous Societies*. Canberra, Australia: Aboriginal Studies Press, 2006.

David-Neel, Alexandra. *With Mystics and Magicians in Tibet*. Oxford, UK: Penguin, 1937.

David, Rosalie. *Handbook to Life in Ancient Egypt*. 1998. Oxford, UK: Oxford University Press, 1999 ed.

Davidson, Hilda Roderick Ellis. *Gods and Myths of Northern Europe*. 1964. Harmondsworth, UK: Penguin, 1990 ed.

Davies, A. Powell. *The Meaning of the Dead Sea Scrolls*. New York, NY: Mentor, 1956.

Davies, Owen. *The Omni Book of the Paranormal and the Mind*. New York, NY: Zebra, 1978.

Davies, William Walter. *The Codes of Hammurabi and Moses*. Cincinnati, OH: Jennings and Graham, 1905.

Davis, F. Hadland. *Myths and Legends of Japan*. 1913. New York, NY: Dover, 1992 ed.

Davis, John J. *Biblical Numerology: A Basic Study of the Use of Numbers in the Bible*. 1968. Grand Rapids, MI: Baker Book House, 1988 ed.

Dawkins, Richard. *The Selfish Gene*. 1976. New York, NY: Oxford University Press, 1978 ed.

———. *The Blind Watchmaker*. New York, NY: W. W. Norton, 1987.

Dawson, Christopher. *Religion and the Rise of Western Culture*. 1950. Garden City, NY: Image Books, 1958 ed.

Day, Michael H. *Fossil Man*. New York, NY: Bantam, 1971.

De Bunsen, Ernest. *The Angel-Messiah of Buddhists, Essenes, and Christians*. London, UK: Longmans, Green, and Co., 1880.

De Chardin, Pierre Teilhard. *The Phenomenon of Man* (Bernard Wall, trans.). 1955. New York, NY: Harper and Row, 1965 ed.

Decker, Ed, and Dave Hunt. *The God Makers*. Eugene, OR: Harvest House Publishers, 1984.

———. *The God Makers II*. Eugene, OR: Harvest House Publishers, 1993.

DeHaan, M. R. *508 Answers to Bible Questions: With Answers to Seeming Bible Contradictions*. 1952. Grand Rapids, MI: Zondervan, 1961 ed.

Delaney, John J. *Pocket Dictionary of Saints*. 1980. New York, NY: Image, 1983 abridged ed.

Dellow, E. L. *Methods of Science*. New York, NY: Universe Books, 1970.

Dentan, Robert C. *The Holy Scriptures*. 1949. Greenwich, CT: Seabury Press, 1953 ed.

Derk, Francis H. *The Names of Christ*. 1969. Minneapolis, MN: Dimension, 1976 ed.

Derlon, Pierre. *The Secrets of the Gypsies*. New York, NY: Ballantine, 1977.

De Rosa, Peter. *Vicars of Christ*. New York, NY: Crown Publishers, 1988.

Desroches-Noblecourt, Christiane. *Tutankhamen*. Boston, MA: New York Graphic Society, 1963.

Deussen, Paul. *The Philosophy of the Upanishads*. Edinburgh, Scotland: T. and T. Clark, 1906.

Development Psychology Today. Del Mar, CA: CRM Books, 1971.

J. Dewey, Arthur, Roy W. Hoover, Lane C. McGaughy, and Daryl D. Schmidt. *The Authentic Letters of Paul: A New Reading of Paul's Rhetoric and Meaning* (Scholars Version). Salem, OR: Polebridge Press, 2010.

Dickens, A. G. *Reformation and Society in Sixteenth-Century Europe*. New York, NY: Harcourt, Brace and World, 1966.

Didron, Adolphe Napoleon. *Christian Iconography: The History of Christian Art in the Middle Ages*. London, UK: George Bell and Sons, 1886.

Dimont, Max I. *Jews, God and History*. New York, NY: Signet, 1962.

Dingle, R. D. (ed.). *The New Testament of Our Lord and Saviour Jesus Christ: According to the Authorized Version*. London, UK: London News, 1847.

Dixon, Dougal. *After Man: A Zoology of the Future*. New York, NY: St. Martin's Press, 1981.

Doane, Thomas William. *Bible Myths and Their Parallels in Other Religions*. New York, NY: Truth Seeker Co., 1882.

Dods, Marcus (ed.). *The Works of Aurelius Augustine, Bishop of Hippo*. 12 vols. Edinburgh, Scotland: T. and T. Clark, 1872-1874.

Donahue, Phil. *The Human Animal*. New York, NY: Fireside, 1985.

Donahue, Phil. *My Own Story*. 1979. New York, NY: Fawcett Crest, 1981 ed.

Donaldson, E. Talbot (trans.). *Beowulf*. New York, NY: W. W. Norton, 1966.

Doré, Gustave. *The Doré Bible Gallery*. Chicago, IL: Bedford, Clarke and Co., 1886.

Doresse, Jean. *The Secret Books of the Egyptian Gnostics: An Introduction to the Gnostic Coptic Manuscripts Discovered at Chenoboskion: Translated from the French by Philip Mairet, with an English Translation and Critical Evaluation of the Gospel According to Thomas*. London, UK: Hollis and Carter, 1960.

Dorner, J. August. *History of the Development of the Doctrine of the Person of Christ* (William L. Alexander, trans.). 2 Vols. Edinburgh, Scotland: T. and T. Clark, 1891.

Dorsey, John M. *Psychology of Emotion: Self Discipline by Conscious Emotional Continence*. Detroit, MI: Center for Health Education, 1971.

Douglas-Klotz, Neil. *Prayers of the Cosmos: Meditations on the Aramaic Words of Jesus*. San Francisco, CA: Harper and Row, 1990.

Douglas, Stephen. *The Redhead Dynasty*. Corona del Mar, CA: NewStyle Communications, 1987.

Dowley, Tim (ed.). *The History of Christianity*. 1977. Oxford, UK: Lion Publishing Co., 1990 ed.

Dowling, Levi. *The Aquarian Gospel of Jesus the Christ: The Philosophical and Practical Basis of the Religion of the Aquarian Age of the World and of the Church Universal*. Los Angeles, CA: Royal Publishing Co., 1909.

Downing, Christine. *The Goddess: Mythological Images of the Feminine*. New York, NY: Crossroad Publishing, 1984.

Doyle, Arthur Conan. *Adventures of Sherlock Holmes*. New York, NY: Harper and Brothers, 1892 ed.

——. *The New Revelation*. (Reprint, Lochlainn Seabrook, ed.) Spring Hill, TN: Sea Raven Press, 2021.

——. *The Coming of the Fairies*. New York, NY: George H. Doran Co., 1921.

——. *The Edge of the Unknown*. 1930. New York, NY: Berkley, 1968 ed.

Drake, Stillman. *Discoveries and Opinions of Galileo*. Garden City, NY: Anchor, 1957.

Drexel, Jeremias. *Zodiacus Christianus*. Munich, Germany: Anna Bergin, 1622.

Dudley, Dean. *History of the First Council of Nice: A World's Christian Convention, A.D. 325*. Boston, MA: C. W. Calkins and Co., 1880.

Dunlap, Samuel Fales. *The Ghebers of Hebron*. 1894. New York, NY: J. W. Bouton, 1898 ed.

Dunn, James D. G. *Unity and Diversity in the New Testament: An Inquiry Into the Character of Earliest Christianity*. Philadelphia, PA: Westminster Press, 1977.

Dunner, Joseph (ed.) *Handbook of World History: Concepts and Issues*. New York, NY: Philosophical Library, 1967.

Dunstan, J. Leslie (ed.). *Protestantism*. New York, NY: Washington Square Press, 1962.

Dupius, Charles F. *The Origin of All Religious Worship*. New Orleans, LA: self-published, 1872.

Dyer, Thomas H. *Pompeii: Its History, Buildings, and Antiquities*. London, UK: Bell and Daldy, 1871.

Easton, Matthew George. *Illustrated Bible Dictionary and Treasury of Biblical History, Biography, Geography, Doctrine, and Literature*. London, UK: T. Nelson and Sons, 1894.

Eban, Abba. *Heritage: Civilization and the Jews*. New York, NY: Summit Books, 1984.

Eddy, Mary Baker Glover. *Science and Health With Key to the Scriptures*. 1875. Boston, MA: self-published, 1889 ed.

Edwards, I. E. S. *The Pyramids of Egypt*. 1947. Harmondsworth, UK: Penguin, 1967 ed.

——. *Tutankhamun: His Tomb and Its Treasures*. 1977. New York, NY: Knopf, 1978 ed.

Edwards, Jonathan. *The Salvation of All Men Strictly Examined*. Boston, MA: C. Ewer and T. Bedlington, 1824.

Edwards, Otis Carl, Jr. *Luke's Story of Jesus*. Philadelphia, PA: Fortress Press, 1981.

Eimerl, Sarel, and Irven DeVore. *The Primates*. New York, NY: Time-Life Books, 1965.

Einstein, Albert. *The World as I See It*. New Jersey: Citadel Press, n.d.

Eisenman, Robert. *Maccabees, Zadokites, Christians, and Qumran: A New Hypothesis of Qumran Origins*. Leiden, The Netherlands: Brill, 1983.

Eisenman, Robert, and Michael Wise. *The Dead Sea Scrolls Uncovered*. Shaftesbury, Dorset, UK: Element Books, 1992.

Elder, Dorothy. *From Metaphysical to Mystical: A Study of the Way*. Denver, CO: Doriel Publishing Co., 1992.

Eliade, Mircea. *Images and Symbols: Studies in Religious Symbolism*. 1952. Princeton, NJ: Princeton University Press, 1991 ed.

———. *Yoga: Immortality and Freedom* (William R. Trask, trans.). 1954. Princeton, NJ: Princeton University Press, 1971 ed.

———. *From Primitives to Zen*. 1967. New York, NY: Harper and Row, 1977 ed.

———. *A History of Religious Ideas*. Vol. 1 (From the Stone Age to the Eleusinian Mysteries). Chicago, IL: University of Chicago Press, 1978.

———. *A History of Religious Ideas*. Vol. 2 (From Gautama Buddha to the Triumph of Christianity). Chicago, IL: University of Chicago Press, 1982.

———. *A History of Religious Ideas*. Vol. 3 (From Muhammad to the Age Reforms). Chicago: University of Chicago Press, 1985.

Eliot, Alexander. *The Universal Myths*. New York, NY: Meridian, 1976.

Ellis, Albert. *The Case Against Religion: A Psychotherapist's View*. Austin, TX: American Atheist Press, n.d.

Ellis, Edwin John, and William Butler Yeats (eds.). *The Works of William Blake: Poetic, Symbolic, and Critical*. Vol. 2. London, UK: Bernard Quaritch, 1893.

Ellis, Peter Berresford. *A Dictionary of Irish Mythology*. 1987. Oxford, UK: Oxford University Press, 1992 ed.

Emerson, Ralph Waldo. *Works of Ralph Waldo Emerson*. London, UK: George Routledge and Sons, 1883.

———. *The Essays of Emerson*. London, UK: Arthur L. Humphreys, 1908.

Encyclopedia Britannica: A New Study of Universal Knowledge. 1768. London, UK: Encyclopedia Britannica, 1955 ed.

Enslin, Morton Scott. *Christian Beginnings*. 1938. New York, NY: Harper and Brothers, 1956 ed.

Erasmus, Desiderius. *Praise of Folly* (1509). Betty Radice, trans. 1971. Harmondsworth, England: Penguin, 1987 ed.

Esslemont, J. E. *Bahá'u'lláh and the New Era: An Introduction to the Baha'i Faith*. 1923. Wilmette, IL: Baha'i Books, 1970 ed.

Eusebius (of Caesarea). *The History of the Church* (c. 315-325). G. A. Williamson, trans; Andrew Louth, ed. 1965. Harmondsworth, England: Penguin, 1989 ed.

———. *The Proof of the Gospel* (W. J. Ferrar, trans.). 2 vols. New York, NY: Macmillan, 1920.

Evans, Bergen. *Dictionary of Mythology*. 1970. New York, NY: Laurel, 1991 ed.

Evans, Elizabeth E. *The Christ Myth: A Study*. New York, NY: The Truth Seeker Co., 1900.

Evans-Wentz, Walter Yeeling. *The Tibetan Book of the Great Liberation, or the Method of Realizing Nirvana Through Knowing the Mind*. 1954. Oxford, UK: Oxford University Press, 1971 ed.

Eyerly, Dean R. *The Face of Jesus*. Mustang, OK: Tate Publishing, 2012.

Faber-Kaiser, Andreas. *Jesus Died in Kashmir: Jesus, Moses and the Ten Lost Tribes of Israel*. London, UK: Gordon and Cremonesi, 1977.

Farmer, David Hugh. *The Oxford Dictionary of Saints*. 1978. Oxford, UK: Oxford University Press, 1992 ed.

Farnese, A. *A Wanderer in Spirit Lands*. Chicago, IL: Progressive Thinker, 1901.

Farrar, Frederic William. *The Life of Christ*. 2 vols. New York: E. P. Dutton and Co., 1877.

Feder, Kenneth L. *Frauds, Myths, and Mysteries: Science and Pseudoscience in Archaeology*. Mountain View, CA: Mayfield Publishing Co., 1990.

Feldman, Louis H., and Gohei Hata (eds.). *Josephus, Judaism, and Christianity*. Leidan, Netherlands: E. J. Brill, 1987.

Fenwick, Peter, and Elizabeth Fenwick. *The Truth in the Light: An Investigation of Over 300 Near-Death Experiences*. 1995. New York, NY: Berkley, 1997 ed.

Ferguson, George. *Signs and Symbols in Christian Art*. 1954. London, UK: Oxford University Press, 1975 ed.

Feuerbach, Ludwig. *The Essence of Christianity* (Maria Evans, trans.). London, UK: Trübner and Co., 1881.

Fichte, Johann Gottlieb. *John Gottlieb Fichte's Popular Works*. London, UK: Trübner and Co., 1873.

Fillmore, Charles. *Metaphysical Bible Dictionary*. Unity Village, MO: Unity School of Christianity, 1931.

Filson, Floyd V. *Opening the New Testament*. 1929. Philadelphia, PA: Westminster Press, 1952 ed.

Filthaut, Theodor. *Church Architecture and Liturgical Reform*. 1965. Baltimore, MD: Helicon Press, 1968 ed.

Finegan, Jack. *Light From the Ancient Past: The Archaeological Background of the Hebrew-Christian Religion*. 1946. 2 vols. Princeton, NJ: Princeton University Press, 1974 ed.

Finger, Ben, Jr. *Concise World History*. New York, NY: Philosophical Library, 1959.

Fischer, Carl. *The Myth and Legend of Greece*. Dayton, OH: George A. Pflaum, 1968.

Flew, Antony. *A Dictionary of Philosophy*. New York, NY: St. Martin's Press, 1979.

Forbes, R. J. *Studies in Ancient Technology* (Vol. 9). Leiden, The Netherlands: Brill, 1964.

Ford, Marvin. *On the Other Side*. Plainfield, NJ: Logos International, 1978.

Fox, George. *George Fox: An Autobiography* (Rufus M. Jones, ed.). Philadelphia, PA: Ferris and Leach, 1904 ed.

Fox, Matthew (ed.) *Western Spirituality: Historical Roots, Ecumenical Routes*. Santa Fe, NM: Bear and Co., 1981.

———. *The Coming of the Cosmic Christ*. New York, NY: Harper and Row, 1988.

———. *Christian Mystics: 365 Readings and Meditations*. Novato, CA: New World Library, 2011.

Fox, Robin Lane. *Pagans and Christians*. New York, NY: Knopf, 1986.

———. *The Unauthorized Version: Truth and Fiction in the Bible*. New York, NY: Knopf, 1991.

Frazer, James George. *Adonis, Attis, Osiris: Studies in the History of Oriental Religion*. London, UK: Macmillan, 1906.

———. *The Golden Bough*. 2 vols. London, UK: Macmillian, 1919.

———. *Folk-lore in the Old Testament: Studies in Comparative Religion, Legend, and Law*. 1918. Single abridged vol. New York, NY: Tudor, 1923 ed.

Freud, Sigmund. *Totem and Taboo: Resemblances Between the Psychic Lives of Savages and Neurotics*. New York, NY: Moffat, Yard and Co., 1918.

———. *The Future of an Illusion*. 1928. New York, NY: W. W. Norton, 1961.

———. *New Introductory Lectures Psychoanalysis*. Lecture no. 35: "A Philosophy of Life," 1932.

———. *Moses and Monotheism*. 1939. New York, NY: Vintage, 1958 ed.

Friend, David, and the editors of *Life*. *The Meaning of Life*. Boston, MA: Little, Brown and Co., 1991.

Frothingham, Octavius Brooks. *The Cradle of the Christ: A Study in Primitive Christianity*. New York, NY: G. P. Putnam's Sons, 1877.

Frye, Albert Myrton, and Albert William Levi. *Rational Belief: An Introduction to Logic*. New York, NY: Harcourt, Brace and Co., 1941.

Furnas, J. C. *The Americans: A Social History of United States (1587-1914)*. New York, NY: G. P. Putnam's Sons, 1969.

Fysh, Frederic. *"The Beast and His Image," or the Pope and the Council of Trent*. London, UK: R. B. Seeley and W. Burnside, 1837.

Gadd, Laurence D. *The World Almanac Book of the Strange 2*. New York, NY: Signet, 1982.

Gaer, Joseph. *The Legend of the Wandering Jew*. New York, NY: Mentor, 1961.

Gantz, Jeffrey (trans.). *Early Irish Myths and Sagas*. 1981. Harmondsworth, UK: Penguin, 1988 ed.

Gardner, Alice. *Studies in John the Scot (Erigena): A Philosopher of the Dark Ages*. London, UK: Henry Frowde, 1900.

Gardner, Joseph L. (ed.). *Great Mysteries of the Past: Experts Unravel Fact and Fallacy Behind the Headlines of History*. Pleasantville, NY: Reader's Digest, 1991.

Gardner, Martin. *Science: Good, Bad, and Bogus*. New York, NY: Avon, 1981.

———. *The New Age: Notes of a Fringe Watcher*. Buffalo, NY: Prometheus, 1988.

Gaskell, G. A. *Dictionary of All Scriptures and Myths*. 1960. New York, NY: Julian Press, 1973 ed.

Gaskin, Stephen. *The Caravan*. New York, NY: Random House, 1972.

———. *Hey Beatnik! This is the Farm Book*. Summertown, TN: The Book Publishing Company, 1974.

———. *Mind at Play*. Summertown, TN: The Book Publishing Company, 1980.

Geiger, Wilhelm, and Friedrich von Spiegel. *The Age of the Avesta and Zoroaster*. London, UK: Henry Frowde, 1886.

Geller, L. D. *Sea Serpents of Coastal New England*. Plymouth, MA: Cape Cod Publications, 1979.

George, Lyman Fairbanks. *The Naked Truth of Jesusism from Oriental Manuscripts*. Pittsburgh, PA: George Book Publishing Co., 1914.

Gibbon, Edward. *Memoirs of My Life* (Betty Radice, ed.). 1788-1791. Harmondsworth, UK: Penguin, 1990.

———. *The History of the Decline and Fall of the Roman Empire*. 8 vols. Paris, France: Baudry's European Library, 1840.

Gibran, Kahlil. *The Prophet*. 1923. New York, NY: Knopf, 1980 ed.

———. *The Broken Wings* (Anthony R. Ferris, trans.). New York, NY: Citadel Press, 1957.

Gimbutas, Marija Alseikait. *The Goddesses and Gods of Old Europe: Myths and Cult Images*. 1974. Berkeley, CA: University of California Press, 1992 ed.

———. *The Civilization of the Goddess: The World of Old Europe*. San Francisco, CA: Harper, 1991.

Ginsburg, Christian David. *The Essenes: Their History and Doctrines*. London, UK: Longman, Green, Longman, Roberts, and Green, 1864.

Godfrey, Laurie R. (ed.). *Scientists Confront Creationism*. New York, NY: W. W. Norton, 1983.

Godwin, Joscelyn. *Arktos: The Polar Myth in Science, Symbolism, and Nazi Survival*. Kempton, IL: Adventures Unlimited Press, 1996.

Goguel, Maurice. *Jesus and the Origins of Christianity*. 2 vols. 1932. New York, NY: Harper and Brothers, 1960 ed.

Golas, Thaddeus. *The Lazy Man's Guide to Enlightenment*. 1971. New York, NY: Bantam, 1980 ed.

Goodrich-Freer, Ada. *Essays in Psychical Research*. London, UK: George Redway, 1899.

Goodspeed, Edgar J. *The Apocrypha: An American Translation*. 1938. New York, NY: Vintage Books, 1959 ed.

———. *How Came the Bible?* Nashville, TN: Abingdon Press, 1940.

Gordon, Stuart. *The Encyclopedia of Myths and Legends*. London, UK: Headline, 1994.

Goring, Rosemary (ed.). *Larousse Dictionary of Beliefs and Religions*. 1992. Edinburgh, Scotland: Larousse, 1995 ed.

Gottlieb, Lynn. *She Who Dwells Within: A Feminist Vision of a Renewed Judaism*. New York, NY: Harper Collins, 1995.

Gould, Stephen Jay. *Ever Since Darwin*. New York, NY: W. W. Norton, 1977.

———. *Hen's Teeth and Horse's Toes*. New York, NY: W. W. Norton, 1983.

———. *Bully for Brontosaurus*. New York, NY: W. W. Norton, 1991.

Graham, Billy. *Approaching Hoofbeats: The Four Horsemen of the Apocalypse*. Minneapolis, MN: Grason, 1983.

———. *Angels: Ringing Assurance That We Are Not Alone*. Nashville, TN: Thomas Nelson, 1996.

Graham, Lloyd M. *Deceptions and Myths of the Bible*. 1975. New York, NY: Citadel Press, 1991, ed.

Grant, Frederick C. (ed.). *Hellenistic Religions: The Age of Syncretism*. Indianapolis, IN: Bobbs-Merrill, 1953.

Grant, Michael. *Jesus: An Historian's Review of the Gospels*. New York, NY: Charles Scribner's Sons, 1977.

———. *Constantine the Great: The Man and His Times*. New York, NY: Charles Scribner's Sons, 1993.

Grant, Michael, and John Hazel. *Who's Who in Classical Mythology*. 1973. New York, NY: Oxford University Press, 1993 ed.

Graves, Frank Pierrepont. *What Did Jesus Teach? An Examination of the Educational Material and Method of the Master*. New York, NY: Macmillan, 1919.

Graves, Kersey. *The World's Sixteen Crucified Saviors, or Christianity Before Christ*. New York, NY: Peter Eckler, 1919.

Graves, Robert. *The White Goddess*. 1948. New York, NY: Noonday Press, 1991 ed.

———. (trans.) *The Golden Ass: The Transformation of Lucius*. 1950. New York, NY: Farrar, Straus and Giroux, 2009 ed.

———. *The Greek Myths*. Vol. 1. 1955. Harmondsworth, UK: Penguin, 1960 ed.

———. *The Greek Myths*. Vol. 2. 1955. Harmondsworth, UK: Penguin, 1990 ed.

Graves, Robert, and Joshua Podro. *The Nazarene Gospel Restored*. London, UK: Cassell and Co., 1953.

Graves, Robert, and Raphael Patai. *Hebrew Myths*. 1964. New York, NY: Anchor, 1989 ed.

Greaves, Helen. *Testimony of Light*. 1969. Saffron Walden, UK: Neville Spearman, 1988 ed.

Greenhouse, Herbert B. *The Book of Psychic Knowledge: All Your Questions Answered*. New York, NY: Mentor, 1973.

Greenstone, Julius H. *The Messiah Idea in Jewish History*. Philadelphia, PA: Jewish Publication Society, 1906.

Greenwood, Samuel. *Footsteps of Israel: From Eden to the City of God*. 1922. Freehold, NJ: Rare Book Co., 1958 ed.

Gregory, Saint, the Great. *Morals on the Book of Job*. 3 vols. Oxford, UK: John Henry Parker, 1847.

Grenfell, Bernard P., and Arthur S. Hunt (eds.). *New Sayings of Jesus and Fragment of a Lost Gospel From Oxyrhyncus*. London, UK: Henry Frowde, 1904.

Grimal, Pierre. *The Penguin Dictionary of Classical Mythology* (A. R. Maxwell-Hyslop, trans.). 1951. Harmondsworth, UK: Penguin, 1990 ed.

Grimes, Nikki. *Portrait of Mary*. New York, NY: Avon, 1994.

Grotjahn, Martin. *The Voice of the Symbol*. Los Angeles, CA: Mara Books, 1971.

Groton, William Mansfield. *The Christian Eucharist and the Pagan Cults*. New York, NY: Longmans, Green, and Co., 1914.

Grun, Bernard. *The Timetables of History*. New York, NY: Touchstone, 1975.

Grusin, Richard A. *Transcendentalist Hermeneutics: Institutional Authority and the Higher Criticism of the Bible*. Durham, NC: Duke University Press, 1991.

Guignebert, Charles. *The Christ*. New York, NY: Citadel, 1968.

Guinness Book of World Records. New York, NY: Bantam, 1990.

Guirand, Felix (ed.) *New Larousse Encyclopedia of Mythology*. 1959. London, UK: Hamlyn Publishing, 1976 ed.

Gulliver, John P. (ed.). *The Complete Works of John Bunyan*. Philadelphia, PA: Bradley, Garretson and Co., 1873.

Hadas, Moses (ed.). *A History of Rome*. Garden City, NY: Doubleday, 1956.

Haley, John Wesley. *An Examination of the Alleged Discrepancies of the Bible*. Andover, MA: Warren F. Draper, 1876.

Hall, J. A. *The Nature of God: A Series of Lectures*. Philadelphia, PA: The Lutheran Publication Society, 1910.

Hall, Manly Palmer. *The Secret Teachings of All Ages*. 1925. Los Angeles, CA: The Philosophical Research Society, 1989 ed.

Hall, Nor. *The Moon and the Virgin: Reflections on the Archetypal Feminine*. New York, NY: Harper and Row, 1980.

Hallo, William W., and William Kelly Simpson. *The Ancient Near East: A History*. New York, NY: Harcourt Brace, 1998.

Hamilton, Edith. *Mythology: Timeless Tales of Gods and Heroes*. 1940. New York, NY: Mentor Books, 1963 ed.

——. *The Roman Way*. 1932. New York, NY: Mentor Books, 1961 ed.

——. *The Greek Way*. 1930. New York, NY: Mentor Books, 1959 ed.

Hampson, Robert Thomas. *Medieval Kalendarium, or Dates, Charters, and Customs of the Middle Ages*. 2 vols. London, UK: Henry Kent Causton and Co., 1841.

Happold, F. C. *Mysticism: A Study and an Anthology*. Harmondsworth, UK: Penguin, 1991.

Hardon, John A. *Pocket Catholic Dictionary*. 1980. New York, NY: Image, 1985 ed.

Harnack, Adolf. *New Testament Studies 2: The Sayings of Jesus—The Second Source of St. Matthew and St. Luke* (J. R. Wilkinson, trans.). London, UK: Williams and Norgate, 1908.

Harpur, James. *The Atlas of Sacred Places: Meeting Points of Heaven and Earth*. New York, NY: Henry Holt, 1994.

Harrington, Daniel J. *Interpreting the New Testament: A Practical Guide*. 1979. Wilmington, DE: Michael Glazier, 1980 ed.

Harris, Marvin. *Our Kind*. New York, NY: Harper and Row, 1989.

Hart, George. *A Dictionary of Egyptian Gods and Goddesses*. 1986. London, UK: Routledge, 1992 ed.

Hartmann, Franz. *In the Pronaos of the Temple of Wisdom: Containing the History of the True and the False Rosicrucians*. London, UK: Theosophical Publishing Society, 1890.

——. *Magic White and Black: Or the Science of Finite and Infinite Life*. London, UK: Kegan Paul, Trench, Trübner, and Co., 1893.

Haskin, Frederic J. *5,000 Answers to Questions*. New York, NY: Grosset and Dunlap, 1933.

Haskins, Susan. *Mary Magdalen: Myth and Metaphor*. New York, NY: Harcourt Brace and Co., 1993.

Hawken, Paul. *The Magic of Findhorn*. New York, NY: Bantam, 1976.

Hawking, Stephen William. *A Brief History of Time: From the Big Bang to Black Holes*. New York, NY: Bantam, 1988.

Hay, Louise L. *You Can Heal Your Life*. 1984. Carlsbad, CA: Hay House, 1987 ed.

Head, Joseph, and S. L. Cranston (eds.). *Reincarnation: An East-West Anthology*. 1961. Wheaton, IL: Quest, 1975 ed.

Heaton, E. W. *Everyday Life in Old Testament Times*. New York, NY: Charles Scribner's Sons, 1956.

Heckethorn, Charles William. *The Secret Societies of All Ages and Countries*. 2 vols. London, UK: James Hogg, 1875.

Hefele, Charles Joseph. *A History of the Councils of the Church, From the Original Documents*. 5 vols. Edinburgh, Scotland: T. and T. Clark, 1871.

Heindel, Max. *The Rosicrucian Cosmo-Conception or Mystic Christianity*. Oceanside, CA: Rosicrucian Fellowship, 1911.

———. *Nature Spirits and Nature Forces*. Oceanside, CA: Rosicrucian Fellowship, 1937.

Helms, Randel. *Gospel Fictions*. Buffalo, NY: Prometheus Books, 1988.

Henry, Caleb Sprague. *A Compendium of Christian Antiquities: Being a Brief View of the Orders, Rites, Laws and Customs of the Ancient Church in the Early Ages*. Philadelphia, PA: Joseph Whetham, 1837.

Herbert W. Armstrong, Keith W. Stump, and John Halford. *The Plain Truth About Christmas*. Pasadena, CA: Worldwide Church of God, 1952, 1985, 1986.

Herm, Gerhard. *The Celts: The People Who Came Out of the Darkness*. New York, NY: St. Martin's Press, 1975.

Herrmann, Samuel O. (ed.). *The Black and Red*, Vol. 21, No. 2, May 1917. (A monthly magazine published by the students of Northwestern College.) Watertown, WI: Northwestern College, 1917.

Hertz, Joseph H. *Sayings of the Fathers: Pirke Aboth*. New York, NY: Behrman House, 1945.

Herzfeld, Ernst E. *Zoroaster and His World*. Princeton, NJ: Princeton University Press, 1947.

Hesiod. *Theogonia; Erga kai Hemerai* (circa 8th Century B.C.) Martin Litchfield West, trans. In English: *Theogony and Work and Days*. 1988. Oxford, UK: Oxford University Press, 1991 ed.

Hesse, Hermann. *Siddhartha*. 1951. New York, NY: Bantam, 1974 ed.

Hewson, William. *The Hebrew and Greek Scriptures Compared With Oriental History, Dialling, Science, and Mythology*. London, UK: Simpkin and Co., 1870.

Hicks, Clive. *Green Man: The Archetype of Our Oneness With the Earth*. London, UK: Harper Collins, 1990.

Higgins, Godfrey. *Anacalypsis, An Attempt to Draw Aside the Veil of the Saitic Isis*. 2 vols. London, UK: Longman, Rees, Orme, Brown, Green and Longman, 1836.

Higginson, Edward. *Astro-Theology; or, The Religion of Astronomy: Four Lectures*. London, UK: E. T. Whitfield, 1855.

Hillman, James. *Insearch: Psychology and Religion*. New York, NY: Charles Scribner's Sons, 1967.

Hinckley, K. C. *A Compact Guide to the Christian Life*. Colorado Springs, CO: NavPress, 1989.

Hinnells, John R. (ed.). *The Penguin Dictionary of Religions*. Harmondsworth, UK: Penguin, 1984.

Hinsie, Leland E., and Robert Jean Campbell. *Psychiatric Dictionary*. New York, NY: Oxford University Press, 1970 ed.

Hislop, Alexander. *The Two Babylons, or The Papal Worship Proved to be the Worship of Nimrod and His Wife*. Edinburgh, Scotland: James Wood, 1862.

Hitching, Francis. *The Mysterious World: An Atlas of the Unexplained*. 1978. New York, NY: Holt, Rinehart and Winston, 1979 ed.

Hodson, Geoffrey. *The Hidden Wisdom in the Holy Bible*. Vol. 1. 1967. Wheaton, IL: Quest/Theosophical Publishing House, 1978 ed.

———. *The Hidden Wisdom in the Holy Bible*. Vol. 2. 1967. Wheaton, IL: Quest/Theosophical Publishing House, 1978 ed.

Hoeller, Stephan A. *Jung and the Lost Gospels: Insights into the Dead Sea Scrolls and the Nag Hammadi Library*. 1989. Wheaton, IL: Quest Books, 1990 ed.

Hoffer, Eric. *The True Believer*. New York, NY: Harper, 1951.

Hoffman, R. Joseph. *Jesus Outside the Gospels*. Buffalo, NY: Prometheus, 1984.

Holden, Joseph M., and Norman Geisler. *The Popular Handbook of Archaeology and the Bible*. Eugene, OR: Harvest House, 2013.

Holdich, Thomas. *Tibet, the Mysterious*. London, UK: London, UK: Alston Rivers, 1906.

Holding, James Patrick. *Shattering the Christ Myth: Did Jesus Not Exist?* Maitland, FL: Xulon Press, 2008.

Holroyd, Stuart. *The Arkana Dictionary of New Perspectives*. Harmondsworth, UK: Arkana, 1989.

Hone, William (ed.). *The Apocryphal New Testament*. London, UK: self-published, 1820.

———. *Ancient Mysteries Described*. London, UK: self-published, 1823.

Hopfe, Lewis M. *Religions of the World*. New York, NY: Macmillan, 1987.

Hopkins, Emma Curtis. *High Mysticism*. New York, NY: Edwin S. Gorham, 1921.

Horne, Herman Harrell. *Jesus the Master Teacher*. New York, NY: Association Press, 1920.

Houvet, Etienne. *Chartres: Guide of the Cathedral*. Paris, France: Houvet-La Crypte, 1972.

Howell, F. Clark. *Early Man*. 1965. New York, NY: Time-Life Books, 1971 ed.

Howells, George. *The Bhagavad Gita and the New Testament: The Internal Relations of Their Fundamental Doctrines*. Cuttack, India: Orissa Mission Press, 1907.

Howitt, William. *The History of the Supernatural: In All Ages and Nations and in All Churches Christian and Pagan, Demonstrating a Universal Faith*. 2 vols. Philadelphia, PA: J. B. Lippincott and Co., 1863.

Hua-Ching, Ni. *The Taoist Inner View of the Universe and the Immortal Realm*. 1979. Malibu, CA: The Shrine of the Eternal Breath of Tao, 1986 ed.

Hughes, Philip. *A Popular History of the Catholic Church*. New York, NY: Macmillan, 1946.

Hume, David. *Dialogues Concerning Natural Religion*. London, UK: n.p., 1779.

Hutchinson, R. W. *Prehistoric Crete*. 1962. Harmondsworth, UK: Penguin, 1968 ed.

Hutchinson, Thomas (ed.). *The Poetical Works of Percy Bysshe Shelley*. London, UK: Henry Frowde, 1905.

Ide, Arthur Frederick. *Unzipped: The Popes Bare All - A Frank Study of Sex and Corruption in the Vatican*. Austin, TX: American Atheist Press, 1987.

———. *Yahweh's Wife: Sex in the Evolution of Monotheism - A Study of Yahweh, Asherah, Ritual Sodomy and Temple Prostitution*. Las Colinas, TX: Monument Press, 1991.

Inge, William Ralph. *Christian Mysticism: Considered in Eight Lectures Delivered Before the University of Oxford*. London, UK: Methuen and Co., 1899.

———. *Personal Idealism and Mysticism*. New York, NY: Longmans, Green, and Co., 1907.

Ingersoll, Robert Green. *Sixty-five Press Interviews with Robert G. Ingersoll*. Austin, TX: American Atheist Press, 1983.

Inman, Thomas. *Ancient Faiths Embodied in Ancient Names*. 2 vols. London, UK: Trübner and Co., 1872.

Ironside, H. A. *Illustrations of Bible Truth*. Chicago, IL: Moody Press, 1945.

Irudayaraj, Xavier (ed.). *Swamy Bede Dayananda: Testimonies and Tributes*. Thannirpalli, South India: Shantivanam Publications, 1994.

Irving, Edward. *The Collected Writings of Edward Irving*. 5 vols. London, UK: Alexander Strahan and Co., 1864.

Jackson, Abraham V. W. *Zoroaster: The Prophet of Ancient Iran*. New York: Columbia University Press, 1898.

Jackson, John G. *Christianity Before Christ*. Austin, TX: American Atheist Press, 1985.

———. *Pagan Origins of the Christ Myth*. Austin, TX: American Atheist Press, n.d.

———. *The Golden Ages of Africa*. Austin, TX: American Atheist Press, 1987.

Jacobi, Jolande. *The Psychology of C. G. Jung*. 1942. New Haven, CT: Yale University Press, 1973 ed.

Jacolliot, M. Louis (trans.). *The Bible in India: Hindoo Origin of Hebrew and Christian Revelation*. New York: Carleton, 1870.

James, William. *The Varieties of Religious Experience*. New York, NY: Mentor, 1902.

Jefferson, Thomas. *The Jefferson Bible: The Life and Morals of Jesus of Nazareth*. 1803. Chicago, IL: N. D. Thompson, 1902 ed.

John, DeWitt. *The Christian Science Way of Life*. Boston, MA: Christian Science Publishing Society, 1962.

Johns, Catherine. *Sex or Symbol? Erotic Images of Greece and Rome.* New York, NY: Routledge, 1982.

Johns, June. *Black Magic Today.* London, UK: New English Library, 1971.

Johnson, Robert A. *Inner Work: Using Dreams and Active Imagination for Personal Growth.* 1986. New York, NY: Harper Collins, 1989 ed.

———. *She: Understanding Feminine Psychology.* 1976. New York, NY: Perennial Library, 1977 ed.

Johnson, William Hallock. *The Christian Faith Under Modern Searchlights.* New York: Fleming H. Revell Co., 1916.

Johnston, Charles. *Bhagavad Gita: The Songs of the Master.* New York, NY: J. J. Little and Ives, 1908.

Johnston, Sarah Iles (ed.). *Religions of the Ancient World: A Guide.* Cambridge, MA: Harvard University Press, 2004.

Jonas, Hans. *The Gnostic Religion: The Message of the Alien God and the Beginnings of Christianity.* 1958. London, UK: Routledge, 1992 ed.

Jones, A. H. M. *Constantine and the Conversion of Europe.* 1948. New York, NY: Collier, 1962 ed.

Jones, Dennis Merritt. *The Art of Being: 101 Ways to Practice Purpose in Your Life.* New York, NY: Penguin, 2008.

Jones, Gwyn. *A History of the Vikings.* 1968. Oxford, UK: Oxford University Press, 1984 ed.

Jones, Rufus Matthew. *Studies in Mystical Religion.* London, UK: Macmillan and Co., 1919.

Jones, William. *Manava Dharma Sastra, or the Institutes of Manu According to the Gloss of Kulluka.* Madras, India: J. Higginbotham, 1863.

Jordan, Louis Henry. *Comparative Religion: Its Adjuncts and Allies.* London, UK: Oxford University Press, 1915.

Jordan, Michael. *Encyclopedia of Gods: Over 2,500 Deities of the World.* New York, NY: Facts on File, 1993.

Josephus, Flavius. *The Works of Flavius Josephus* (William Whiston, trans.). Philadelphia, PA: David McKay, 1850.

Joyce, T. Athol, and N. W. Thomas. *Women of All Nations.* New York, NY: Metro Publications, 1942.

Jukes, Andrew. *The Types of Genesis Briefly Considered As Revealing the Development of Human Nature.* London, UK: Longmans, Green, and Co., 1885.

Julian of Norwich. *Revelations of Divine Love* (Clifton Wolters, trans.). 1373. Harmondsworth, UK: Penguin, 1966.

Jung, Carl Gustav. *Psychology and Religion.* 1938. New Haven, CT: Yale University Press, 1961 ed.

———. *Man and His Symbols.* 1964. New York, NY: Dell, 1968 ed.

Kapadia, Shapurji Asponiaryi. *The Teachings of Zoroaster and the Philosophy of the Parsi Religion.* London, UK: John Murray, 1913.

Kaplan, Justin. *Walt Whitman: A Life.* New York, NY: Simon and Shuster, 1980.

Kavanagh, Morgan. *Origin of Language and Myths.* 2 vols. London, UK: Sampson Low, Son, and Marston, 1871.

Kavanaugh, James. *A Modern Priest Looks at His Outdated Church.* New York, NY: Trident Press, 1967.

———. *The Birth of God.* New York, NY: Trident Press, 1969.

Kawaguchi, Ekai. *Three Years in Tibet.* Madras, India: Theosophical Publishing Society, 1909.

Keable, Robert. *The Great Galilean.* Boston, MA: Little, Brown and Co., 1929.

Keck, Leander E. *Taking the Bible Seriously.* New York, NY: Association Press, 1962.

Kee, Howard Clark. *The Origins of Christianity: Sources and Documents.* Englewood Cliffs, NJ: Prentice-Hall, 1973.

Keller, Werner. *The Bible As History.* 1956. New York, NY: Bantam, 1980 ed.

Kelly, John Norman Davidson. *Early Christian Doctrines.* 1960. San Francisco, CA: Harper and Row, 1978 ed.

Kelly, Sean, and Rosemary Rogers. *Saints Preserve Us! Everything You Need to Know About Every Saint You'll Ever Need.* New York, NY: Random House, 1993.

Kennett, David. *Pharaoh: Life and Afterlife of a God.* New York, NY: Walker and Co., 2008.

Kerr, Adrian R. J. *Ancient Egypt and Us: The Impact of Ancient Egypt on the Modern World.* Ft. Myers, FL: Ferniehirst Trading, 2008.

Kertzer, Morris N. *What Is a Jew?* 1953. New York, NY: Macmillan, 1971 ed.

Khan, Pir Vilayat Inayat. *Toward the One*. London, UK: Harper Colophon, 1974.

King, Charles W. *The Gnostics and Their Remains, Ancient and Medieval*. London, UK: Bell and Daldy, 1864.

King, Jawara D. *The Awakening of Global Consciousness: A Guide to Self-Realization and Spirituality*. Bloomington, IN: AuthorHouse, 2010.

King, Karen L. *Images of the Feminine in Gnosticism*. 1988. Harrisburg, PA: Trinity Press, 2000 ed.

Kingsbury, Jack Dean. *Matthew: Structure, Christology, Kingdom*. 1975. Philadelphia, PA: Fortress Press, 1978 ed.

Kingsford, Anna, and Edward Maitland. *The Perfect Way; or, The Finding of Christ*. London, UK: Leadenhall Press, 1890.

Kingsley, Charles. *The Works of Charles Kingsley, Vol. 26: The Water of Life*. London, UK: Macmillan and Co., 1881.

Kirk, George E. *A Short History of the Middle East: From the Rise of Islam to Modern Times*. New York, NY: Praeger, 1959.

Kirk, G. S. *The Nature of the Greek Myths*. 1974. Harmondsworth, UK: Penguin, 1978 ed.

Kirk, Robert. *The Secret Commonwealth of Elves, Fauns, and Fairies: A Study in Folk-lore and Psychical Research*. 1691. London, UK: David Nutt, 1893 ed.

Kitto, John (ed.). *A Cyclopedia of Biblical Literature*. 2 vols. Edinburgh, Scotland: Adam and Charles Black, 1851.

——. *An Illustrated History of the Holy Bible*. Norwich, CT: Henry Bill, 1869.

Kloppenborg, John S. *The Formation of Q: Trajectories in Ancient Wisdom Collections*. 1987. Minneapolis, MN: Fortress Press, 2007 ed.

——. *Q Parallels: Synopsis, Critical Notes, and Concordance*. Sonoma, CA: Polebridge Press, 1988.

Knight, Richard Payne. *An Inquiry Into the Symbolic Language of Ancient Art and Mythology*. 1818. London, UK: Black and Armstrong, 1836 ed.

Knox, John. *The History of the Reformation of Religion in Scotland*. C. 1560. London, UK: Andrew Melrose, 1905.

Köstenberger, Andreas J. *John*. Grand Rapids, MI: Baker Publishing, 2004.

Köstenberger, Andreas J., L. Scott Kellum, and Charles L. Quarles. *The Cradle, the Cross, and the Crown: An Introduction to the New Testament*. Nashville, TN: B. and H., 2009.

Krippner, Stanley, and Daniel Rubin (eds.). *The Kirlian Aura: Photographing the Galaxies of Life*. New York, NY: Anchor Books, 1974.

Krishna, Gopi. *The Real Nature of Mystical Experience*. New York, NY: New Concepts, 1978.

——. *Kundalini in Time and Space*. New Delhi, India: Kundalini Research and Publication Trust, 1979.

Krishnamurti, Jiddu. *The First and Last Freedom*. 1954. Wheaton, IL: Quest, 1968 ed.

——. *Think on These Things* (D. Rajagopal, ed.). 1964. New York, NY: Perennial Library, 1970 ed.

——. *Talks and Dialogues*. 1968. New York, NY: Avon, 1970 ed.

——. *On Relationship*. New York, NY: Harper Collins, 1992.

Krutch, Joseph Wood. *Henry David Thoreau*. 1948. New York, NY: William Morrow and Co., 1974 ed.

Kuehl, Nancy L. *Becoming Christian: The Demise of the Jesus Movement*. Eugene, OR: Resource, 2014.

Kuhn, Alvin Boyd. *Who is This King of Glory?: A Critical Study of the Christos-Messiah Tradition*. Elizabeth, NJ: Academy Press, 1944.

——. *Lost Light: An Interpretation of Ancient Scriptures*. Minneapolis, MN: Filiquarian, 2007.

Kul, Djwal. *Intermediate Studies of the Human Aura*. 1974. Colorado Springs, CO: Summit University Press, 1976 ed.

Kümmel, W. G. *The New Testament: The History of the Investigation of Its Problems*. Nashville, TN: Abingdon, 1972.

Küng, Hans. *Christianity: Essence, History, and Future*. New York, NY: Continuum, 1995.

Küng, Hans, and Jürgen Moltmann (eds.). *Conflicts About the Holy Spirit*. New York, NY: Seabury Press, 1979.

Kyle, Melvin Grove. *Moses and the Monuments: Light from Archaeology on Pentateuchal Times*. Oberlin, OH: Bibliotheca Sacra Co., 1920.

Ladd, George Trumbull. *The Philosophy of Religion*. 2 vols. 1905. New York, NY: Charles

Scribner's Sons, 1909 ed.

Lamsa, George M. *The Holy Bible From Ancient Eastern Manuscripts*. 1933. Philadelphia, PA: A. J. Holman Co., 1957 ed.

——. *Idioms in the Bible Explained and A Key to the Original Gospels*. 1931. New York, NY: Harper Collins, 1985 ed.

Landis, Benson Y. *An Outline of the Bible Book by Book*. 1963. New York, NY: Barnes and Noble, 1970 ed.

Lange, Johann Peter. *The Life of Jesus Christ: A Complete Critical Examination of the Origin, Contents, and Connection of the Gospels*. 4 vols. Edinburgh, Scotland: T. and T. Clark, 1872.

Langford, Norman F. *Fire Upon the Earth: The Story of the Christian Church*. Philadelphia, PA: Westminster Press, 1950.

Lao-Tsu. *Tao Te Ching*. New York, NY: Vintage Books, 1972.

Lapide, Pinchas E. *Three Popes and the Jews*. New York, NY: Hawthorne Books, 1967.

Larousse Encyclopedia of Archeology. 1969. New York, NY: Crescent Books, 1987 ed.

Larson, Bob. *Satanism: The Seduction of America's Youth*. Nashville, TN: Thomas Nelson, 1989.

Lash, John Lamb. *Not In His Image: Gnostic Vision, Sacred Ecology, and the Future of Belief*. White River Junction, VT: Chelsea Green, 2006.

Lasne, Sophie, and André Pascal Gaultier. *A Dictionary of Superstitions: From the Ridiculous to the Sublime*. Englewood Cliffs, NJ: Prentice-Hall, 1984.

Lass, Abraham H., David Kiremidjian, and Ruth M. Goldstein. *The Dictionary of Classical, Biblical, and Literary Allusions*. New York, NY: Fawcett Gold Medal, 1987.

Law, William. *The Works of the Reverend William Law, M.A., Sometime Fellow of the Emmanuel College, Cambridge*. 9 vols. 1762. Brockenhurst, Hampshire, UK: 1893 ed.

Layton, Bentley. *The Gnostic Scriptures: Ancient Wisdom for the New Age*. New York, NY: Doubleday, 1987.

Leakey, Richard E. *The Making of Mankind*. New York, NY: E. P. Dutton and Co., 1981.

Leakey, Richard E., and Roger Lewin. *Origins*. New York, NY: E. P. Dutton and Co., 1977.

——. *Origins Reconsidered: In Search of What Makes Us Human*. New York, NY: Doubleday, 1992.

Learsi, Rufus. *Israel: A History of the Jewish People*. 1949. Cleveland, OH: Meridian, 1966 ed.

Leboyer, Frederick. *Birth Without Violence*. 1975. New York, NY: Knopf, 1978 ed.

Lee, Arthur Patterson. *The Controversial Jesus and the Critics*. Toronto, Canada: Clements Publishing, 2002.

Lee, Dal. *Understanding the Occult: Secrets of Psychic Phenomena Revealed*. New York, NY: Paperback Library, 1969.

Lee, Jae Hyun. *Paul's Gospel in Romans: A Discourse Analysis of Rom. 1:16-8:39*. Leiden, The Netherlands, Brill, 2010.

Leek, Sybil. *The Complete Art of Witchcraft*. New York, NY: Signet, 1971.

Leeming, David Adams. *The World of Myth*. New York, NY: Oxford University Press, 1990.

Leggat, P. O., and D. V. Leggat. *The Healing Wells: Cornish Cults and Customs*. Kernow, Cornwall, UK: Truran, 1987.

Legge, Francis. *Forerunner and Rivals of Christianity: Being Studies in Religious History From 330 B.C. to 330 A.D.* 2 vols. Cambridge, UK: Cambridge University Press, 1915.

Leishman, Thomas Linton. *Our Ageless Bible: From Early Manuscripts to Modern Versions*. 1939. New York, NY: Thomas Nelson and Sons, 1962 ed.

——. *The Continuity of the Bible: The Gospels*. Boston, MA: Christian Science Publishing Society, 1976.

Leloup, Jean-Yves. *The Gospel of Philip: Jesus, Mary Magdalene, and the Gnosis of the Sacred Union*. Rochester, VT: Inner Traditions, 2004.

Lemesurier, Peter. *The Armageddon Script: Prophecy in Action*. Rockport, MA: Element, 1993.

Lenz, Frederick. *Lifetimes: True Accounts of Reincarnation*. New York, NY: Fawcett Crest, 1979.

Lerner, Gerda. *The Creation of Patriarchy*. 1986. Oxford, UK: Oxford University Press, 1987 ed.

Lessa, William A., and Evon Z. Vogt. *Reader in Comparative Religion: An Anthropological Approach*. New York, NY: Harper and Row, 1979.

Lewis, Abram Herbert. *Paganism Surviving In Christianity*. New York, NY: G. P. Putnam's Sons, 1892.

Lewis, C. S. *Mere Christianity*. 1943. New York, NY: Macmillan, 1973 ed.

———. *The Problem of Pain*. New York, NY: Collier, 1962.

Lewis, Harvey Spencer. *Mansions of the Soul: The Cosmic Conception*. 1930. San Jose, CA: Ancient Mystical Order Rosae Crucis (AMORC), 1969 ed.

———. *The Secret Doctrine of Jesus*. 1937. San Jose, CA: Rosicrucian Press, 1954 ed.

Lewis, I. M. *Ecstatic Religion: An Anthropological Study of Spirit Possession and Shamanism*. 1971. Harmondsworth, UK: Penguin, 1975 ed.

Levy, Rosalie Marie. *Heavenly Friends: A Saint For Each Day*. Boston, MA: Daughters of St. Paul, 1956.

Liddon, Henry Parry. *Sermons Preached Before the University of Oxford*. Oxford, UK: James Parker and Co., 1869.

Lieberman, E. James. *Acts of Will: The Life and Work of Otto Rank*. New York, NY: The Free Press, 1985.

Liebowitz, Michael R. *The Chemistry of Love*. 1983. New York, NY: Berkley Books, 1984 ed.

Life—How Did It Get Here? By Evolution or Creation? Brooklyn, NY: Watchtower Bible and Tract Society of New York, 1985.

Lillie, Arthur. *Buddhism in Christendom, or Jesus, the Essene*. London, UK: Kegan Paul, Trench and Co., 1887.

———. *The Influence of Buddhism on Primitive Christianity*. London, UK: Swan Sonnenschein and Co., 1893.

Lilly, John C. *The Human Biocomputer*. London: Abacus, 1967.

Lindsay, Hal. *The Rapture: Truth or Consequences*. New York, NY: Bantam, 1983.

Lindsay, Hal, and Carole C. Carlson. *The Late Great Planet Earth*. 1970. New York, NY: Bantam, 1990 ed.

———. *There's a New World Coming: A Prophetic Odyssey*. Santa Ana, CA: Vision House, 1973.

Link, John R. *Help in Understanding the Bible*. Valley Forge, PA: Judson Press, 1974.

Little, L. Gilbert. *Nervous Christians*. Chicago, IL: Moody Press, 1956.

Littleton, C. Scott (ed.). *Mythology: The Illustrated Anthology of World Myth and Storytelling*. London, UK: Duncan Baird, 2002.

———. (ed.) *Gods, Goddesses, and Mythology*. 11 vols. Tarrytown, NY: Marshall Cavendish, 2005.

Livingstone, Elizabeth Anne (ed.). *The Concise Oxford Dictionary of the Christian Church*. Oxford, UK: Oxford University Press, 1990 ed.

Llewelyn, Robert. *All Shall Be Well: The Spirituality of Julian of Norwich for Today*. Mahwah, NJ: Paulist Press, 1982.

Loar, Julie. *Goddesses For Every Day: Exploring the Wisdom and Power of the Divine Feminine Around the World*. Novato, CA: New World Library, 2011.

Lockyer, Herbert. *All the Women of the Bible*. 1967. Grand Rapids, MI: Zondervan, 1988 ed.

Locy, William A. *The Story of Biology*. Garden City, NY: Garden City Publishing Co., 1925.

Lohse, Eduard. *The New Testament Environment*. 1971. Nashville, TN: Abingdon, 1974 ed.

Loomis, Roger Sherman. *The Grail: From Celtic Myth to Christian Symbol*. 1963. Princeton, NJ: Princeton University Press, 1991 ed.

Lorberbaum, Yair. *Disempowered King: Monarchy in Classical Jewish Literature*. London, UK: Continuum International Publishing Group, 2011.

Lord, John. *The Old Pagan Civilizations*. New York, NY: Fords, Howard, and Hulbert, 1888.

Louis, David. *More Fascinating Facts*. New York, NY: The Ridge Press, 1979.

Lucas, Alfred, and John Richard Harris. *Ancient Egyptian Materials and Industries*. 1962. Mineola, NY: Dover, 1999 ed.

Ludlow, Daniel H. *Encyclopedia of Mormonism: The History, Scripture, Doctrine, and Procedure of the Church of Jesus Christ of Latter Day Saints*. New York, NY: Macmillan, 1992.

Lundy, John Patterson. *Monumental Christianity, or the Art and Symbolism of the Primitive Church As Witnesses and Teachers of the One Catholic Faith and Practice*. New York, NY: J. W. Bouton, 1876.

Luomanen, Petri. *Recovering Jewish-Christian Sects and Gospels*. Leiden, The Netherlands: Brill, 2012.

Lurker, Manfred. *Dictionary of Gods and Goddesses, Devils and Demons* (G. L. Campbell, trans.). 1984. London, UK: Routledge, 1988 ed.

———. *The Gods and Symbols of Ancient Egypt* (Barbara Cumming, trans.). 1974. London, UK: Thames and Hudson, 1984 ed.

Lyle, Anthony. *Ancient History: A Revised Chronology—An Updated Version of Ancient History Based on New Archaeology* (Vol. 1). Bloomington, IN: AuthorHouse, 2012.

Lynch, Frances. *Megalithic Tombs and Long Barrows in Britain.* 1997. Princes Risborough, UK: Shire Publications, 2004 ed.

MacCulloch, John Arnott. *Comparative Theology.* London, UK: Methuen and Co., 1902.

MacGregor, Geddes. *Reincarnation in Christianity: A New Vision of the Role of Rebirth in Christian Thought.* 1978. Wheaton, IL: Theosophical Publishing House, 1989 ed.

MacGregor, George Hogarth Carnaby. *The New Testament Basis of Pacifism.* 1936. New York, NY: Fellowship of Reconciliation, 1954 ed.

MacIntyre, Alisdair (ed.). *Hume's Ethical Writings.* London, UK: Collier, 1965.

Mack, Burton L. *The Lost Gospel: The Book of Q and Christian Origins.* New York, NY: Harper Collins, 1993.

Mackay, Robert William. *A Sketch of the Rise and Progress of Christianity.* London, UK: John Chapman, 1854.

Mackey, Albert Gallatin. *The Symbolism of Freemasonry: Illustrating and Explaining its Science and Philosophy, its Legends, Myths, and Symbols.* New York, NY: Clark and Maynard, 1869.

Maclaren, Alexander. *Sermons Preached in Manchester.* London, UK: Macmillan and Co., 1873.

——. *St. Paul's Epistle to the Romans.* New York, NY: A. C. Armstrong and Son, 1909.

Mader, Sylvia S. *Inquiry Into Life.* 1976. Dubuque, IA: William C. Brown Publishers, 1988 ed.

Magee, Bryan. *Philosophy and the Real World: An Inroduction to Karl Popper.* 1973. La Salle, IL: Open Court Publishing Co., 1990 ed.

Magli, Giulio. *Mysteries and Discoveries of Archaeoastronomy: From Giza to Easter Island.* 2005. New York, NY: Copernicus Books, 2009 ed.

Magoulias, Harry J. *Byzantine Christianity: Emperor, Church and the West.* Chicago, IL: Rand McNally and Co., 1970.

Maharshi, Ramana. *The Spiritual Teaching of Ramana Maharshi.* Berkeley, CA: Shambala, 1972.

Maitland, Edward. *Anna Kingsford: Her Life, Letters, Diary, and Work.* 2 vols. London, UK: George Redway, 1896.

Manniche, Lise. *Sexual Life in Ancient Egypt.* 2002. London, UK: Kegan Paul, 2002.

Man's Place in Evolution. Cambridge, UK: British Museum of Natural History/Cambridge University Press, 1980.

Man's Search for God. Brooklyn, NY: Watchtower Bible and Tract Society of New York, 1990.

Marshall, George N. *Challenge of a Liberal Faith.* 1966. Boston, MA: Unitarian Universalist Association, 1975 ed.

Marshall, I. Howard. *Luke: Historian and Theologian.* 1970. Grand Rapids, MI: Zondervan, 1974 ed.

——. *I Believe in the Historical Jesus.* Vancouver, BC: Regent College Publishing, 2001.

Martello, Leo Louis. *Weird Ways of Witchcraft.* 1969. San Francisco, CA: Red Wheel, 2011 ed.

Martin, Joel, and Patricia Romanowski. *We Don't Die: George Anderson's Conversations With the Other Side.* New York, NY: G. P. Putnam's Sons, 1988.

Marty, Martin E. (ed.). *New Directions in Biblical Thought.* New York, NY: Association Press, 1960.

Massey, Gerald. *Ancient Egypt: The Light of the World - A Work of Reclamation and Restitution.* 12 vols. London, UK: T. Fisher Unwin, 1907.

Matthews, Caitlín. *Celtic Devotional: Daily Prayers and Blessings.* New York, NY: Harmony, 1996.

Maurice, Thomas. *The History of Hindostan.* 2 vols. London UK: self-published, 1820.

May, Rollo. *The Cry for Myth.* New York, NY: W. W. Norton, 1991.

McBee, Silas (ed.). *The Constructive Quarterly: A Journal of the Faith, Work and Thought of Christendom.* Vol. 1, March to December, 1913. New York, NY: George H., Doran Co., 1913.

McCannon, Tricia. *Jesus: The Explosive Story of the 30 Lost Years and the Ancient Mystery Religions.* Charlottesville, VA: Hampton Roads Publishing, 2010.

McClelland, Norman C. *Encyclopedia of Reincarnation and Karma.* Jefferson, NC: McFarland and Co., 2010.

McColman, Carl. *The Big Book of Christian Mysticism: The Essential Guide to Contemplative Spirituality.* Charlottesville, VA: Hampton Roads Publishing, 2010.

McConkie, Bruce R. *Mormon Doctrine.* 1966. Salt Lake City, UT: Bookcraft, 1992 ed.

McDonnell, Thomas P. *A Thomas Merton Reader.* Garden City, NY: Image Books, 1974.

McFague, Sally. *Metaphorical Theology*. Philadelphia, PA: Fortress Press, 1982.

McGovern, Patrick E. *Ancient Wine: The Search for the Origins of Viniculture*. 2003. Princeton, NJ: Princeton University Press, 2007 ed.

McGowan, Chris. *In the Beginning....* Buffalo, NY: Prometheus Books, 1984.

McIntosh, Jane R. *Ancient Mesopotamia: New Perspectives*. Santa Barbara, CA: ABC-Clio, 2005.

McKenzie, J. Hewat. *Spirit Intercourse: Its Theory and Practice*. New York, NY: Mitchell Kennerley, 1917.

McKenzie, John L. *Dictionary of the Bible*. New York, NY: Collier, 1965.

Mead, Frank S. *Handbook of Denominations in the United States*. 1951. Nashville: Abingdon Press, 1989 ed.

Mead, George Robert Stow. *Orpheus*. London, UK: Theosophical Publishing Society, 1896.

———. (ed.). *Pistis Sophia: A Gnostic Gospel*. London, UK: Theosophical Publishing Society, 1896.

———. *Did Jesus Live 100 B.C.?* London, UK: Theosophical Publishing Society, 1903.

———. *Fragments of a Faith Forgotten: Some Short Sketches Among the Gnostics*. 1900. Theosophical Publishing Society, 1906 ed.

———. *Thrice-Greatest Hermes: Studies in Hellenistic Theosophy and Gnosis*. 3 vols. London, UK: Theosophical Publishing Society, 1906.

———. (trans.) *The Hymn of Jesus: Echos From the Gnosis*. 1907. Wheaton, IL: Theosophical Publishing House, 1973 ed.

Mead, Margaret. *Male and Female*. 1949. New York, NY: Mentor, 1959 ed.

Meeks, Wayne A. *The Origins of Christian Morality: The First Two Centuries*. New Haven, CT: Yale University Press, 1993.

Meissner, William W. *Psychoanalysis and Religious Experience*. New Haven, CT: Yale University Press, 1984.

Mendelssohn, Kurt. *The Riddle of the Pyramids*. 1974. London, UK: Thames and Hudson, 1986 ed.

Menzies, Allan (ed.). *The Ante-Nicene Fathers: Translations of the Fathers Down to A.D. 325* (original supplement to the American edition). 10 vols. New York, NY: The Christian Literature Co., 1896.

Mercatante, Anthony S. (ed.). *The Harper Book of Christian Poetry*. New York, NY: Harper and Row, 1972.

Merriam-Webster's Collegiate Encyclopedia. Springfield, MA: Merriam-Webster, 2000.

Metford, J. C. J. *Dictionary of Christian Lore and Legend*. London, UK: Thames and Hudson, 1983.

Metzger, Bruce M. *A Text of the New Testament: Its Transmission, Corruption, and Restoration*. Oxford, UK: Oxford University Press, 1968.

———. *The Text of the New Testament: Its Transmission, Corruption, and Restoration*. New York, NY: Oxford University Press, 1968.

Metzger, Bruce M., and Michael D. Coogan (eds.). *The Oxford Companion to the Bible*. Oxford, UK: Oxford University Press, 1993.

Meyer, Marvin W. *The Secret Teachings of Jesus: Four Gnostic Gospels*. New York, NY: Random House, 1984.

———. *The Ancient Mysteries: A Sourcebook*. New York, NY: Harper and Row, 1987.

Miller, Robert J. (ed.). *The Complete Gospels* (annotated scholars version). San Francisco, CA: Polebridge Press, 1994.

Mills, Lawrence H. *Zarathushtra, Philo, the Achaemenids, and Israel*. Chicago, IL: The Open Court Publishing Co., 1906.

Milman, Henry Hart (ed.). *The Life of Edward Gibbon, Esq.* London, UK: John Murray, 1839.

Milton, John. *Selected Prose* (Malcom W. Wallace, ed.). 1641-1659. London, UK: Oxford University Press, 1959.

Mish, Frederick (ed.). *Webster's Ninth New Collegiate Dictionary*. 1828. Springfield, MA: Merriam-Webster, 1984.

Modi, Jivanji Jamshedji. *The Religious System of the Parsis: A Paper*. Bombay, India: Bombay Education Society's Press, 1903.

Mollenkott, Virginia Ramey. *The Divine Feminine: The Biblical Imagery of God as Female*. 1983. New York, NY: Crossroad, 1993 ed.

Moltmann, Jürgen. *The Crucified God: The Cross of Christ as the Foundation and Criticism of Christian Theology*. New York, NY: Harper and Row, 1973.

Monaghan, Patricia. *The Book of Goddesses and Heroines*. 1981. St. Paul, MN: Llewellyn Publications, 1990 ed.

Monier-Williams, Monier. *Buddhism, in its Connexion with Brahmanism and Hinduism, and in its Contrast With Christianity*. New York: Macmillan and Co., 1889.

Monk, Robert C., Walter C. Hofheinz, Kenneth T. Lawrence, Joseph D. Stamey, Bert Affleck, and Tetsunao Yamamori. *Exploring Religious Meaning*. Englewood Cliffs, NJ: Prentice-Hall, 1973.

Montagu, Ashley. *The Natural Superiority of Women*. 1952. New York, NY: Collier, 1992 ed.

———. *Man: His First Million Years*. New York, NY: Signet, 1962.

Montefiore, Hugh. *Paul the Apostle*. London, UK: Fount, 1981.

Montgomery, James A. (ed.). *Religions of the Past and Present*. Philadelphia, PA: J. B. Lippincott, 1918.

Moor, Edward. *The Hindu Pantheon*. Madras, India: J. Higginbotham, 1864.

Morgan, Elaine. *The Descent of Woman*. 1972. New York, NY: Bantam, 1973 ed.

———. *The Aquatic Ape*. New York, NY: Stein and Day, 1982.

Morris, Desmond. *The Naked Ape*. New York, NY: Dell, 1967.

———. *Bodywatching: A Field Guide to the Human Species*. New York, NY: Crown, 1985.

Morris, Henry M. *The Bible and Modern Science*. 1951. Chicago, IL: Moody Press, 1956 ed.

Morrison, Sarah Lyddon. *The Modern Witch's Spellbook*. Secaucus, NJ: Lyle Stuart, 1971.

Morrow, Louis Laravoire. *My Catholic Faith: A Manual of Religion*. 1949. Kenosha, WI: My Mission House, 1961 ed.

Moscati, Sabatino. *The Face of the Ancient Orient: Near Eastern Civilization in Pre-Classical Times*. 1960. Mineola, NY: Dover, 2001 ed.

Moses, William Stainton. *Spirit Teachings*. London, UK: London Spiritualist Alliance, 1907.

Mueller, David L. *Karl Barth*. Waco, TX: Word Books, 1972.

Muilenburg, James. *The Way of Israel: Biblical Faith and Ethics*. 1961. New York, NY: Harper and Row, 1965 ed.

Müller, Carl Otfried. *Introduction to a Scientific System of Mythology* (John Leitch, trans.) London, UK: Longman, Brown, Green, and Longmans, 1844.

Müller, Friedrich Max (trans.). *The Upanishads*. Oxford, UK: Clarendon Press, 1879.

———. *Theosophy or Psychological Religion*. London, UK: Longmans, Green, and Co., 1893.

———. *Ramakrishna: His Life and Sayings*. London, UK: Longmans, Green, and Co., 1898.

——— (ed.). *The Sacred Books of the East, Translated by Various Oriental Scholars*. 50 vols. Oxford, UK: Clarendon Press, 1900.

Mullins, E. Y., and H. W. Tribble. *The Baptist Faith*. Nashville, TN: Southern Baptist Convention, 1935.

Murdock, D. M. *Christ in Egypt: The Horus-Jesus Connection*. Seattle, WA: Stellar House, 2009.

———. *Did Moses Exist? The Myth of the Israelite Lawgiver*. Seattle, WA: Stellar House, 2014.

Murnane, William J. *The Penguin Guide to Ancient Egypt*. 1983. Harmondsworth, UK: Penguin, 1984 ed.

Murray, Gilbert (ed. and trans.). *The Bacchae of Euripides*. New York, NY: Longmans, Green, and Co., 1915.

Myer, Isaac. *Qabbalah: The Philosophical Writings of Solomon Ben Yehudah Ibn Gebirol*. Philadelphia, PA: self-published, 1888.

Narasu, Pokala Lakshmi. *The Essence of Buddhism*. Madras, India: Srinivasa Varadachari and Co., 1907.

Nath, Samir. *Encyclopaedic Dictionary of Buddhism*. 3 vols. New Delhi, India: Sarup and Sons, 1998.

Neander, Augustus. *General History of the Christian Religion and Church*. 2 vols. 1847. Boston, MA: Crocker and Brewster, 1854 ed.

Neher, Andrew. *The Psychology of Transcendence*. 1980. New York, NY: Dover, 1990 ed.

Neihardt, John G. *Black Elk Speaks*. 1932. New York, NY: Pocket Books, 1973 ed.

Neill, Stephen. *The Interpretation of the New Testament, 1861-1961*. 1964. Oxford, UK: Oxford University Press, 1970 ed.

———. *What We Know About Jesus*. 1970. Grand Rapids, MI: William B. Eermans Publishing Co., 1972 ed.

Nelson's New Compact Illustrated Bible Dictionary. Nashville, TN: Thomas Nelson,1978.

Neumann, Erich. *The Great Mother: An Analysis of the Archetype*. New York, NY: Pantheon, 1955.

Newall, Venetia. *The Encyclopedia of Witchcraft and Magic*. A and W Visual Library, 1974.

Nicholson, Edward Byron. *The Gospel According to the Hebrews*. London, UK: C. Kegan Paul and Co., 1879.

Nietzche, Friedrich. *Thus Spoke Zarathustra* (1883-1885). R. J. Hollingdale, trans. 1961. Harmondsworth, England: Penguin, 1972 ed.

Notovitch, Nicolas. *The Unknown Life of Jesus Christ* (Alexina Loranger, trans.). Chicago, IL: Rand, McNally and Co., 1894.

Novak, Peter. *Original Christianity: A New Key to Understanding the Gospel of Thomas and Other Lost Scriptures*. Charlottesville, VA: Hampton Roads Publishing, 2005.

O'Brien, Isidore. *The Life of Christ*. 1937. Paterson, NJ: St. Anthony Guild Press, 1950 ed.

O'Dea, Thomas F. *The Mormons*. Chicago: University of Chicago Press, 1957.

Odent, Michael. *Water and Sexuality*. Harmondsworth, England: Arkana, 1990.

Oldenberg, Hermann. *Buddha: His Life, His Doctrine, His Order* (William Hoey, trans.). London, UK: Williams and Norgate, 1882.

Olson, Carl (ed.). *The Book of Goddess Past and Present: An Introduction to Her Religion*. New York, NY: Crossroad, 1989.

Otto, Rudolf. *Mysticism East and West: A Comparative Analysis of the Nature of Mysticism*. Wheaton, IL: Quest, 1987.

Ottum, Bob (ed.). *A Day in the Life of the Amish*. Greendale, WI: Reiman, 1994.

Owen, John B. *The Eighteenth Century: 1714-1815*. 1974. New York, NY: W. W. Norton, 1976 ed.

Oxford English Dictionary (compact edition). 2 vols. 1928. Oxford, UK: Oxford University Press, 1979 ed.

Oxford Society of Historical Theology. *The New Testament in the Apostolic Fathers*. Oxford, UK: Clarendon Press, 1905.

Pagels, Elaine. *The Gnostic Gospels*. 1979. New York, NY: Vintage Books, 1981 ed.

———. *Adam, Eve, and the Serpent: Sex and Politics in Early Christianity*. 1988. New York, NY: Vintage Books, 1989 ed.

———. *The Gnostic Paul: Gnostic Exegesis of the Pauline Letters*. London, UK: Continuum, 1992.

Paine, Lauran. *Witches in Fact and Fantasy*. 1971. New York, NY: Taplinger Publishing Co., 1972 ed.

Paine, Thomas. *The Age of Reason: Being an Investigation of True and Fabulous Theology*. 1794. New York, NY: D. M. Bennett, 1877 ed.

Paley, William. *The Works of William Paley*. Edinburgh, Scotland: Peter Brown and T. and W. Nelson, 1827.

Parker, Theodore. *The Transient and Permanent in Christianity*. Boston, MA: American Unitarian Association, 1908.

Parkes, James. *Whose Land? A History of the Peoples of Palestine*. 1940. Harmondsworth, UK: Penguin, 1979 ed.

———. *The Conflict of the Church and the Synagogue: A Study in the Origins of Antisemitism*. New York, NY: Meridian, 1961.

Parrinder, Geoffrey. *Encountering World Religions: Questions of Religious Truth*. New York, NY: Crossroad, 1987.

———. *Avatar and Incarnation: The Divine in Human Form in the World's Religions*. Oxford, UK: Oneworld, 1997.

Parsons, Albert Ross. *New Light From the Great Pyramid*. New York, NY: Metaphysical Publishing Co., 1893.

Pasachoff, Jay M. *Astronomy: From the Earth to the Universe*. Philadelphia: W. B. Saunders Co., 1979.

Patai, Raphael. *The Hebrew Goddess*. 1967. Detroit, MI: Wayne State University Press, 1990 ed.

Patterson, Stephen J., and James M. Robinson. *The Fifth Gospel: The Gospel of Thomas Comes of Age*. Harrisburg, PA: Trinity Press International, 1998.

Paul, John, II. *Crossing the Threshold of Hope*. New York, NY: Knopf, 1994.

Paulsen, Kathryn. *The Complete Book of Magic and Witchcraft*. 1970. New York, NY: Signet, 1980 ed.

Pearson, Carol S. *Awakening the Heroes Within: Twelve Archetypes to Help Us Find Ourselves and*

Transform Our World. New York, NY: Harper San Francisco, 1991.

Peel, Robert. *Spiritual Healing in a Scientific Age*. San Francisco, CA: Harper and Row, 1988.

Peers, E. Allison (ed. and trans.). *Dark Night of the Soul* (Saint John of the Cross). 16th Century. 1959. New York, NY: Image, 1990 ed.

Pegis, Anton C. (ed.) *Introduction to Saint Thomas Aquinas*. 1945. New York, NY: Modern Library, 1948 ed.

Pelikan, Jaroslav (ed.). *The World Treasury of Modern Religious Thought*. Boston, MA: Little, Brown and Co., 1990.

Pennick, Nigel. *The Pagan Book of Days: A Guide to the Festivals, Traditions, and Sacred Days of the Year*. Rochester, VT: Destiny Books, 1992.

Pennock, Michael. *The New Testament: The Good News of Jesus*. Notre Dame, IN: Ave Maria Press, 1982.

Perowne, Stewart. *Roman Mythology*. 1969. Twickenham, UK: Newnes Books, 1986 ed.

Peters, F. E. *Children of Abraham: Judaism, Christianity, Islam*. 1982. Princeton, NJ: Princeton University Press, 1984 ed.

Petrie, William Matthew Flinders. *The Pyramids and Temples of Gizeh*. London, UK: Field and Tuer, 1883.

Pfleiderer, Otto. *The Philosophy of Religion on the Basis of Its History*. 2 vols. London, UK: Williams and Norgate, 1886.

———. *The Early Christian Conception of Christ: Its Significance and Value in the History of Religion*. London, UK: Williams and Norgate, 1905.

———. *The Development of Christianity*. London, UK: T. Fisher Unwin, 1910.

Philo of Alexandria. *The Works of Philo Judaeus, the Contemporary of Josephus* (C. D. Yonge, trans.). 4 vols. London, UK: Henry G. Bohn, 1855.

Pike, Albert. *Morals and Dogma of the Ancient and Accepted Scottish Rite of Freemasonry, Prepared for the Supreme Council of the Thirty-Third Degree for the Southern Jurisdiction of the United States and Published by Its Authority*. Charleston, SC: L. H. Jenkins, 1871.

Pike, James A. *If This Be Heresy*. New York, NY: Harper and Row, 1967.

Platt, Rutherford Hayes (ed.). *The Lost Books of the Bible and the Forgotten Books of Eden*. World Bible Publishers, 1926.

Plumb, J. H. *The Italian Renaissance: A Concise Survey of Its History and Culture*. 1961. New York, NY: Harper and Row, 1965 ed.

Plutarch. *Fall of the Roman Empire* (Rex Warner, trans.). C. 100 C.E. Harmondsworth, UK: Penguin, 1972.

———. *Plutarch's Morals: Theosophical Essays* (Charles W. King, trans.). London, UK: George Bell and Sons, 1898.

Pollock, Frederick. *Spinoza: His Life and Philosophy*. London, UK: C. Kegan Paul and Co., 1880.

Ponder, Catherine. *The Dynamic Laws of Prayer*. Marina Del Rey, CA: DeVorss and Co., 1987.

Porter, Stanley E. (ed.). *Handbook to Exegesis of the New Testament*. Leiden, The Netherlands: Brill, 1997.

Potter, Charles Francis. *The Lost Years of Jesus Revealed*. 1958. New York, NY: Fawcett, 1962 ed.

Powell, John. *The Christian Vision: The Truth That Sets Us Free*. Allen, TX: Argus Communications, 1984

Powers, Joseph M. *Spirit and Sacrament: The Humanizing Experience*. New York, NY: Seabury Press, 1973.

Prabhavananda, Swami. *The Sermon on the Mount According to Vedanta*. New York, NY: Mentor, 1972.

Prahbupada, A. C. Bhaktivedanta Swami. *Bhagavad Gita As It Is*. 1968. Los Angeles, CA: The Bhaktivedanta Book Trust, 1981 ed.

———. *The Science of Self Realization*. 1971. Los Angeles, CA: The Bhaktivedanta Book Trust, 1981 ed.

———. *Beyond Birth and Death*. Los Angeles, CA: The Bhaktivedanta Book Trust, 1979.

———. *Message of Godhead*. Los Angeles, CA: The Bhaktivedanta Book Trust, 1990.

———. *Renunciation Through Wisdom*. Los Angeles, CA: International Society for Krishna Consciousness, 1992.

Preller, Victor. *Divine Science and the Science of God: A Reformulation of Thomas Aquinas*. Princeton,

NJ: Princeton University Press, 1967.

Price, Ira Maurice. *The Ancestry of Our English Bible: An Account of the Bible Versions, Texts, and Manuscripts*. Philadelphia, PA: The Sunday School Times Co., 1907.

Price, Theron Douglas. *Europe Before Rome: A Site-by-Site Tour of the Stone, Bronze, and Iron Ages*. New York, NY: Oxford University Press, 2013.

Prichard, Marianna Nugent, and Norman Young Prichard. *Back to the Sources*. Boston, MA: United Church Press, 1964.

Priestley, Joseph. *The Theological and Miscellaneous Works of Joseph Priestly* (John T. Rutt, ed.). 1786. 25 vols. London, UK: G. Smallfield, 1817-1831 ed.

Pritchard, James B. *Palestinian Figurines in Relation to Certain Goddesses Known Through Literature*. New Haven, CT: American Oriental Society, 1943.

Prophet, Elizabeth Clare. *The Lost Years of Jesus: Documentary Evidence of Jesus' 17-year Journey to the East*. Gardiner, MT: Summit University Press, 1984.

Prophet, Elizabeth Clare, and the Staff of Summit University. *Walking With the Master: Answering the Call of Jesus*. Gardiner, MT: Summit Lighthouse Library, 2002.

Prophet, Elizabeth Clare, and Erin L. Prophet. *Reincarnation: The Missing Link in Christianity*. Livingston, MT: Summit University Press, 1997.

Prophet, Mark L., and Elizabeth Clare Prophet. *The Lost Teachings of Jesus*. Livingston, MT: Summit University Press, 1986.

Pryse, James Morgan. *The Restored New Testament*. London, UK: John M. Watkins, 1914.

Qualls-Corbett, Nancy. *The Sacred Prostitute: Eternal Aspect of the Feminine*. Toronto, Canada: Inner City Books, 1988.

Radner, Daisie, and Michael Radner. *Science and Unreason*. Belmont, CA: Wadsworth Publishing Co., 1982.

Raftery, Barry. *Pagan Celtic Ireland: The Enigma of the Irish Iron Age*. London, UK: Thames and Hudson, 1994.

Ragg, Lonsdale, and Laura Ragg (eds. and trans.). *The Gospel of Barnabas: Edited and Translated From the Italian Ms. in the Imperial Library at Vienna*. Oxford, UK: Clarendon Press, 1907.

Ramacharaka, Yogi. *A Series of Lessons in Mystic Christianity*. Chicago, IL: Yogi Publication Society, 1907.

Ramm, Bernard L. *Hermeneutics*. 1967. Grand Rapids, MI: Baker Book House, 1988 ed.

Rampa, T. Lobsang. *The Third Eye: The Autobiography of a Tibetan Lama*. 1956. New York, NY: Ballantine, 1993 ed.

Randolph, Thomas Jefferson (ed.). *Memoir, Correspondence, and Miscellanies, From the Papers of Thomas Jefferson*. Charlottesville, VA: F. Carr and Co., 1829.

Rawlinson, George. *The History of Herodotus*. 4 vols. New York, NY: D. Appleton and Co., 1889.

Read, Anne. *Edgar Cayce on Jesus and His Church*. 1970. New York, NY: Warner, 1972 ed.

Reed, Graham. *The Psychology of Anomalous Experience*. Buffalo, NY: Prometheus Books, 1988.

Reed, Henry (ed.). *The Complete Poetical Works of William Wordsworth*. Philadelphia, PA: James Kay Jr. and Brother, 1837.

Reilly, Patrician Lynn. *A God Who Looks Like Me: Discovering a Woman-Affirming Spirituality*. New York, NY: Ballantine, 1995.

Renan, M. Ernest. *The Life of Jesus*. London, UK: Trübner and Co., 1864.

———. *Studies of Religious History and Criticism*. New York: Carleton, 1864.

Reyes, E. Christopher. *In His Name: Who Wrote the Gospels?* Bloomington, IN: Trafford, 2014.

Ricciotti, Giuseppe. *The Life of Christ*. Milwaukee, WI: Bruce Publishing, 1947.

Rich, Benjamin E. (ed.) *Latter Day Saints Southern Star*. Vol. 2. Chattanooga, TN: The Southern States Mission, 1900.

Richard, Suzanne (ed.). *Near-Eastern Archaeology: A Reader*. Winona Lake, IN: Eisenbrauns, 2003.

Richards, Le Grand. *A Marvelous Work and a Wonder*. Salt Lake City, UT: Deseret Book Company, 1950.

Richardson, Cyril C. (ed.). *Early Church Fathers*. New York, NY: Collier, 1970.

Ridderbos, Herman. *Paul: An Outline of His Theology* (John R. De Witt, trans.). 1966. Grand Rapids, MI: Eerdmans, 1975 ed.

Riedel, Eunice, Thomas Tracy, and Barbra D. Moskowitz. *The Book of the Bible*. New York, NY: William Morrow and Co., 1979.

Ritchie, Jean. *Death's Door: True Stories of Near-Death Experiences.* New York, NY: Dell, 1996.

Robaldo, John E. (cathechetical notes by). *The Holy Gospel of Our Lord and Savior Jesus Christ.* Boston, MA: St. Paul Editions, 1984.

Roberts, Alexander, and James Donaldson (eds.). *The Ante-Nicene Fathers: Translations of the Fathers Down to A.D. 325* (American reprint of the Edinburgh edition). 10 vols. New York, NY: Charles Scribner's Sons, 1899.

Roberts, Jane. *Seth Speaks: The Eternal Validity of the Soul.* New York, NY: Bantam, 1972.

Roberts, Mark D. *Can We Trust the Gospels? Investigating the Reliability of Matthew, Mark, Luke, and John.* Wheaton, IL: Crossway, 2007.

Robertson, John Mackinnon. *Christianity and Mythology.* London, UK: Watts and Co., 1900.

———. *Pagan Christs: Studies in Comparative Hierology* (2nd ed.) London, UK: Watts and Co., 1911.

Robertson, Pat. *The Secret Kingdom.* Nashville, TN: Thomas Nelson, 1982.

Robinson, James M. (ed.). *The Nag Hammadi Library in English.* 1978. New York, NY: Harper Collins, 1988 ed.

Robinson, Lytle. *Edgar Cayce's Story of the Origin and Destiny of Man.* 1972. New York, NY: Berkley, 1984 ed.

Robinson, Paschal. *The Writings of Saint Francis of Assisi.* Philadelphia, PA: The Dolphin Press, 1905.

Roddy, Lee, and Charles E. Sellier Jr. *In Search of Historic Jesus.* 1960. New York, NY: Bantam, 1979 ed.

Roerich, Nicholas. *Heart of Asia.* New York: Roerich Museum Press, 1929.

———. *Altai-Himalaya: A Travel Diary.* New York: Frederick A. Stokes Co., 1929.

Rogo, D. Scott. *Man Does Survive Death: The Welcoming Silence.* 1973. Secaucus, NJ: Citadel Press, 1977 ed.

Romer, John. *Testament.* New York, NY: Henry Holt and Co., 1988.

Ross, Floyd H., and Tynette Hills. *The Great Religions By Which Men Live.* 1956. New York, NY: Premier, 1961 ed.

Rosten, Leo. *A Guide to the Religions of America.* New York, NY: Simon and Schuster, 1955.

Rouse, W. H. D. *Gods, Heroes and Men of Ancient Greece.* New York, NY: Mentor, 1957.

Rubin, Zick, and Elton B. McNeil. *The Psychology of Being Human.* New York, NY: Harper and Row, 1983.

Rudolph, Kurt. *Gnosis: The Nature and History of Gnosticism.* 1977. Edinburgh, Scotland: T. and T. Clark, 1983 ed.

Rudrananda, Swami. *Spiritual Cannibalism.* New York, NY: Links Books, 1973.

Ruether, Rosemary Radford. *The Radical Kingdom: The Western Experience of Messianic Hope.* New York, NY: Harper and Row, 1970.

Rufus, Anneli S., and Kristan Lawson. *Goddess Sites: Europe.* New York, NY: Harper Collins, 1991.

Runciman, Steven. *A History of the Crusades, Vol. 1: The First Crusade.* 1951. New York, NY: Harper Torchbooks, 1964 ed.

Runes, Dagobert D. (ed.). *Dictionary of Judaism.* 1959. New York, NY: Citadel Press, 1991 ed.

Russell, Bertrand. *A History of Western Philosophy.* 1945. New York, NY: Touchstone, 1972 ed.

———. *Why I Am Not a Christian.* 1930. New York, NY: Touchstone, 1957 ed.

Russell, Charles Taze. *Studies in the Scriptures: The Finished Mystery.* Brooklyn, NY: People's Pulpit Association, 1917.

Rutherford, Ward. *Celtic Mythology: The Nature and Influence of Celtic Myth—From Druidism to Arthurian Legend.* 1987. New York, NY: Sterling Publishing Co., 1990 ed.

Sagan, Carl. *Cosmos.* New York, NY: Random House, 1980.

Sagan, Carl, and Ann Druyan. *Shadows of Forgotten Ancestors: A Search for Who We Are.* New York, NY: Random House, 1992.

Salm, René. *The Myth of Nazareth: The Invented Town of Jesus.* Parsipanny, NJ: American Atheist Press, 2008.

Salmonson, Jessica Amanda. *The Encyclopedia of Amazons: Women Warriors from Antiquity to the Modern Era.* New York, NY: Paragon House, 1991.

Sanders, E. P. *The Historical Figure of Jesus.* Harmondsworth, UK: Penguin, 1993.

Sanford, John A. *Dreams: God's Forgotten Language.* Philadelphia, PA: J. B. Lippincott, 1968.

———. *The Kingdom Within.* New York, NY: Paulist Press, 1970.

Sastri, Hosakote Krishna. *South-Indian Images of Gods and Goddesses.* Madras, India: Madras

Government Press, 1916.

Sayce, Archibald Henry. *The Religions of Ancient Egypt and Babylonia*. Edinburgh, Scotland: T. and T. Clark, 1903.

Schaberg, Jane. *The Resurrection of Mary Magdalene: Legends, Apocrypha, and the Christian Testament*. New York, NY: Continuum, 2004.

Schleiermacher, Friedrich Daniel Ernst. *On Religion: Speeches to its Cultured Despisers*. 1799. (John Oman, trans.) London, UK: Kegan Paul, Trench, Trübner, and Co., 1893.

——. *A Critical Essay on the Gospel of St. Luke*. London, UK: John Taylor, 1825.

——. *The Christian Faith*. 1830. (English translation; H. R. Mackintosh and J. S. Stewart, eds.). Edinburgh, Scotland: T and T Clark, 1928.

Schonfield, Hugh J. *Secrets of the Dead Sea Scrolls*. 1957. New York, NY: Perpetua, 1960 ed.

——. *The Authentic New Testament*. New York, NY: Mentor, 1958.

——. *The Passover Plot*. New York, NY: Bernard Geis Associates, 1965.

——. *Those Incredible Christians*. New York, NY: Bernard Geis Associates, 1968.

——. *The Jesus Party*. New York, NY: Macmillan, 1974.

Schopenhauer, Arthur. *The World as Will and Idea*. 4 vols. 1876. London, UK: Kegan Paul, Trench, Trübner, and Co., 1906 ed.

Schwartz, Howard. *Gabriel's Palace: Jewish Mystical Tales*. New York, NY: Oxford University Press, 1993.

Schweitzer, Albert. *The Quest of the Historical Jesus: A Critical Study of its Progress From Reimarus to Wrede*. (W. Montgomery, trans.) 1906. London, UK: Adam and Charles Black, 1910 ed.

——. *The Mystery of the Kingdom of God: The Secret of Jesus' Messiahship and Passion*. New York, NY: Dodd, Mead and Co., 1914.

——. *Out of My Life and Thought: An Autobiography*. 1933. New York, NY: Henry Holt and Co., 1949 ed.

Scott-Moncrieff, Philip David. *Paganism and Christianity in Ancient Egypt*. Cambridge, UK: University Press, 1913.

Scrivener, Frederick H. (Intro.). *A Full Collation of the Codex Sinaiticus With the Received Text of the New Testament*. Cambridge, UK: Deighton, Bell, and Co., 1864.

Seabrook, Lochlainn. *Aphrodite's Trade: The Hidden History of Prostitution Unveiled*. 1994. Franklin, TN: Sea Raven Press, 2011 ed.

——. *The Goddess Dictionary of Words and Phrases: Introducing a New Core Vocabulary for the Women's Spirituality Movement*. 1997. Franklin, TN: Sea Raven Press, 2010 ed.

——. *Britannia Rules: Goddess-Worship in Ancient Anglo-Celtic Society - An Academic Look at the United Kingdom's Matricentric Spiritual Past*. 1999. Franklin, TN: Sea Raven Press, 2010 ed.

——. *The Book of Kelle: An Introduction to Goddess-Worship and the Great Celtic Mother-Goddess Kelle, Original Blessed Lady of Ireland*. 1999. Franklin, TN: Sea Raven Press, 2010 ed.

——. *UFOs and Aliens: The Complete Guidebook*. Spring Hill, TN: Sea Raven Press, 2005.

——. *Christmas Before Christianity: How the Birthday of the "Sun" Became the Birthday of the "Son."* Franklin, TN: Sea Raven Press, 2010.

——. *Everything You Were Taught About the Civil War is Wrong, Ask a Southerner!* 2010. Franklin, TN: Sea Raven Press, 2024 ed.

——. *Jesus and the Law of Attraction: The Bible-Based Guide to Creating Perfect Health, Wealth, and Happiness Following Christ's Simple Formula*. Franklin, TN: Sea Raven Press, 2013.

——. *The Bible and the Law of Attraction: 99 Teachings of Jesus, the Apostles, and the Prophets*. Franklin, TN: Sea Raven Press, 2013.

——. *Christ Is All and In All: Rediscovering Your Divine Nature and the Kingdom Within*. Franklin, TN: Sea Raven Press, 2014.

——. *Jesus and the Gospel of Q: Christ's Pre-Christian Teachings as Recorded in the New Testament*. Franklin, TN: Sea Raven Press, 2014.

——. *Seabrook's Bible Dictionary of Traditional and Mystical Christian Doctrines*. Spring Hill, TN: Sea Raven Press, 2016.

——. *The Martian Anomalies: A Photographic Search for Intelligent Life on Mars*. Spring Hill, TN: Sea Raven Press, 2022.

——. *Secrets of Celebrity Surnames: An Onomastic Dictionary of Famous People*. Cody, WY: Sea Raven Press, 2023.

——. *Mysterious Invaders: Twelve Famous 20th-Century Scientists Confront the UFO Phenomenon*. Cody, WY: Sea Raven Press, 2024.

——. *Your Soul Lives Forever: Documented Victorian Case Studies Proving Consciousness Survives Death*. Cody, WY: Sea Raven Press, 2024.

Segal, Alan F. *Paul the Convert: the Apostolate and Apostasy of Saul the Pharisee*. New Haven, CT: Yale University Press, 1990.

Seiss, Joseph Augustus. *The Gospel in the Stars; or, Primeval Astronomy*. Philadelphia, PA: E. Claxton and Co., 1882.

Sell, Henry T. *Bible Study By Books*. Chicago, IL: Fleming H. Revell Co., 1896.

Seton-Williams, Veronica, and Peter Stock. *Blue Guide: Egypt*. London, UK: Ernest Benn Ltd., and New York, NY: W. W. Norton, 1983.

Sewall, Charles G. *The Bible and Its Books*. Nashville, TN: Abingdon Press, 1941.

Shah, Idries. *The Sufis*. 1964. Garden City, NY: Anchor, 1971 ed.

Shanks, Hershel. *Understanding the Dead Sea Scrolls*. New York, NY: Random House, 1992.

Shapley, Harlow (ed.). *Science Ponders Religion*. New York, NY: Appleton-Century-Crofts, 1960.

Sharpe, Samuel. *Egyptian Mythology and Egyptian Christianity: With Their Influence on the Opinions of Modern Christendom*. London, UK: Carter and Co., 1896.

Sheehan, Thomas. *The First Coming: How the Kingdom of God Became Christianity*. 1986. New York, NY: Vintage, 1988 ed.

Shemesh, A. Ben (pseudonym). *Was Enoch a Solar Myth? A Contribution to Biblical Solar Mythology*. Oxford, UK: self-published, 1885.

Shenkman, Richard. *Legends, Lies, and Cherished Myths of American History*. New York, NY: Harper and Row, 1988.

Shillington, V. George. *Jesus and Paul Before Christianity: Their World and Work in Retrospect*. Eugene, OR: Cascade, 2011.

Shinn, Florence Scovel. *The Game of Life and How to Play It*. Camarillo, CA: DeVorss, 1925.

Silk, Mark. *Spiritual Politics: Religion and American Since World War II*. New York, NY: Touchstone, 1988.

Sinetar, Marsha. *Ordinary People as Monks and Mystics: Lifestyles for Spiritual Wholeness*. Mahwah, NJ: Paulist Press, 2007.

Singh, Kirpal. *Man! Know Thyself*. 1954. Anaheim, CA: Divine Science of the Soul, 1988 ed.

——. *The Crown of Life: A Study in Yoga*. Delhi, India: Ruhani Satsang, 1974.

Sire, James W. *Scripture Twisting: 20 Ways the Cults Misread the Bible*. Downers Grove, IL: InterVarsity Press, 1980.

Sjöö, Monica, and Barbara Mor. *The Great Cosmic Mother: Rediscovering the Religion of the Earth*. San Francisco, CA: Harper and Row, 1987.

Skarin, Annalee. *Ye Are Gods*. New York, NY: Philosophical Library, 1952.

Skelton, Robin, and Margaret Blackwood. *Earth, Air, Fire, Water: Pre-Christian and Pagan Elements in British Songs, Rhymes and Ballads*. Harmondsworth, England: Arkana, 1990.

Skinner, Tom. *If Christ is the Answer, What Are the Questions?* 1974. Grand Rapids, MI: Zondervan, 1980 ed.

Slater, Philip E. *The Glory of Hera: Greek Mythology and the Greek Family*. Boston, MA: Beacon Press, 1968.

Sleater, Matthew. *A Complete History of the Holy Bible*. 2 vols. Dublin, Ireland: J. Charles, 1810.

Smith, Andrew Phillip. *The Gospel of Philip: Annotated and Explained*. Woodstock, VT: Skylight Paths, 2005.

Smith, Edward Reaugh. *The Disciple Whom Jesus Loved: Unveiling the Author of John's Gospel*. Great Barrington, MA: Anthroposophic Press, 2000.

Smith, Huston. *The Religions of Man*. 1958. New York, NY: Perennial Library, 1965 ed.

Smith, Morton. *Clement of Alexandria and a Secret Gospel of Mark*. Cambridge, MA: Harvard University Press, 1973.

Smith, Morton, and R. Joseph Hoffmann (eds.). *What the Bible Really Says*. Buffalo, NY: Prometheus, 1989.

Smith, Susy. *Out-of-Body Experiences for the Millions*. Los Angeles, CA: Dell, 1969.

Smith, William. *Nelson's Quick Reference Bible Dictionary*. Nashville, TN: Thomas Nelson, 1993.

Spalding, Baird Thomas. *Life and Teachings of the Masters of the Far East*. 5 vols. 1924. Marina Del

Rey, CA: DeVorss, 1964-1976 ed.

Spence, Lewis. *An Encyclopedia of Occultism*. New York, NY: Dodd, Mead and Co., 1920.

Spivey, Robert A., and D. Moody Smith. *Anatomy of the New Testament: A Guide to Its Structure and Meaning*. 1969. New York, NY: Macmillan, 1982 ed.

Spivey, Thomas Sawyer. *The Last of the Gnostic Masters*. Beverly Hills, CA: self-published, 1926.

Spong, John Shelby. *Rescuing the Bible from Fundamentalism: A Bishop Rethinks the Meaning of Scripture*. 1991. San Francisco, CA: Harper San Francisco, 1992 ed.

Springett, Bernard H. *Secret Sects of Syria and the Lebanon: A Consideration of the Their Origin, Creeds and Religious Ceremonies, and Their Connection With and Influence Upon Modern Freemasonry*. London, UK: George Allen and Unwin, 1922.

Staniforth, Maxwell (trans.). *Early Christian Writings: The Apostolic Fathers*. 1968. Harmondsworth, UK: Penguin, 1984 ed.

Stanley, Thomas. *The Chaldaick Oracles of Zoroaster and His Followers: With the Expositions of Pletho and Psellus*. London, UK: Thomas Dring, 1661.

Starbuck, Edwin Diller. *The Psychology of Religion: An Empirical Study of the Growth of Religious Consciousness*. London, UK: Walter Scott, 1900.

Stearn, Jess. *Edgar Cayce: The Sleeping Prophet*. 1967. New York, NY: Bantam, 1971 ed.

Stebbins, J. E. *Moses and the Prophets: Christ and the Apostles; Fathers and Martyrs*. Hartford, CT: Hurlbut, Kellogg and Co., 1861.

Steiger, Brad. *In My Soul I Am Free: The Incredible Paul Twitchell Story*. Menlo Park, CA: IWP, 1968.

———. *Encounters of the Angelic Kind*. Cottonwood, AZ: Esoteric Publications, 1979.

Stein, Diane. *The Goddess Book of Days*. 1988. Freedom, CA: The Crossing Press, 1992 ed.

Stein, Gordon. *The Encyclopedia of Unbelief*. Vol. 1, A-K. Buffalo, NY: Prometheus Books, 1985.

———. *The Encyclopedia of Unbelief*. Vol. 2, L-Z. Buffalo, NY: Prometheus Books, 1985.

Steinberg, Milton. *Basic Judaism*. 1947. San Diego, CA: Harvest, 1975 ed.

Steiner, Rudolf. *From Buddha to Christ*. Spring Valley, NY: Anthroposophic Press, 1978.

Stendahl, Krister. *Paul Among Jews and Gentiles*. Philadelphia, PA: Fortress Press, 1976.

Stern, Karl. *The Third Revolution: A Study of Psychiatry and Religion*. 1954. Garden City, NY: Image Books, 1961 ed.

Stevenson, Leslie. *Seven Theories of Human Nature*. 1974. Oxford, UK: Oxford University Press, 1987 ed.

Stewart, Thomas Milton. *Symbolic Teaching: Or, Masonry and Its Message*. 1914. Cincinnati, OH: Stewart and Kidd Co., 1917 ed.

Stirling, William. *The Canon: An Exposition of the Pagan Mystery Perpetuated in the Cabala as the Rule of All Arts*. London, UK: Elkin Mathews, 1897.

Stokes, Mack B. *The Bible in the Wesleyan Heritage*. 1979. Nashville, TN: Abingdon, 1981 ed.

Stone, Merlin. *When God was a Woman*. San Diego, CA: Harvest, 1976.

———. *Ancient Mirrors of Womanhood: A Treasury of Goddess and Heroine Lore From Around the World*. 1979. Boston, MA: Beacon Press, 1990 ed.

Stott, John R. W. *The Cross of Christ*. Downers Grove, IL: InterVarsity Press, 1986.

Strauss, David Friedrich. *The Life of Jesus Critically Examined* (George Eliot, trans.). 1 vol. complete. London, UK: Swan Sonnenschein, 1892.

———. *The Old Faith and the New: A Confession* (Mathilde Blind, trans.). London, UK: Asher and Co., 1874.

Streep, Peg. *Sanctuaries of the Goddess: The Sacred Landscapes and Objects*. Boston, MA: Bullfinch Press, 1994.

Strobel, Lee. *The Case for Christ: A Journalist's Personal Investigation of the Evidence for Jesus*. Grand Rapids, MI: Zondervan, 1998.

Strong, James. *Strong's Exhaustive Concordance of the Bible*. 1890. Nashville, TN: Abingdon Press, 1975 ed.

Suarès, Carlo. *The Cipher of Genesis: The Original Code of the Qabala as Applied to the Scriptures*. Berkeley, CA: Shambala, 1970.

Stuart, J. P. (ed.). *Popery Adjudged; or, The Roman Catholic Church Weighed in the Balance of God's Word and Found Wanting*. Boston, MA: Redding and Co., 1854.

Stuart, Micheline. *The Tarot: Path to Self Development*. Boulder, CO: Shambhala, 1977.

Stuart, Moses. *A Commentary on the Apocalypse*. 2 vols. Andover, MA: Allen, Morrill and Wardwell,

1845.

Sutphen, Dick. *You Were Born Again to Be Together*. New York, NY: Pocket Books, 1976.

Sutphen Dick, and Trenna Sutphen. *The Master of Life Manual*. Scottsdale, AZ: Valley of the Sun, 1980.

Suzuki, Shunryu. *Zen Mind, Beginner's Mind: Informal Talks on Zen Meditation and Practice*. Boulder, CO: Shambhala, 1993.

Swedenborg, Emanuel. *The Apocalypse Revealed, Wherein Are Disclosed the Arcana There Foretold, Which Have Heretofore Remained Concealed*. 2 vols. New York, NY: American Swedenborg Printing and Publishing Society, 1855 ed.

——. *Arcana Celestia: The Heavenly Mysteries Contained in the Holy Scripture*. 12 vols. London, UK: The Swedenborg Society, 1861 ed.

——. *The Heavenly Arcana Disclosed Which Are in the Sacred Scripture or the Word of the Lord*. 2 vols. 1749. New York, NY: American Swedenborg Printing and Publishing Society, 1896 ed.

——. *The True Christian Religion Containing The Universal Theology of the New Church*. 1771. New York, NY: American Swedenborg Printing and Publishing Society, 1906 ed.

Sykes, Egerton. *Who's Who in Non-Classical Mythology*. 1952. New York, NY: Oxford University Press, 1993 ed.

Szekely, Edmond Bordeaux. *The Essene Gospel of Peace*. Vol. 1. 1924. Cartago, Costa Rica: International Biogenic Society, 1978 ed.

——. *The Essene Gospel of Peace: The Unknown Books of the Essenes*. Vol. 2. 1924. San Diego, CA: Academy Books, 1974 ed.

——. *The Essene Gospel of Peace: Lost Scrolls of the Essene Brotherhood*. Vol. 3. 1924. Cartago, Costa Rica: International Biogenic Society, 1978 ed.

——. *The Essene Teachings of Zarathustra*. San Diego, CA: Academy of Creative Living, 1970.

——. *The Essenes: By Josephus and his Contemporaries*. 1970. San Diego, CA: Academy of Creative Living, 1972 ed.

——. *The Evolution of Human Thought*. Cartago, Costa Rica: International Biogenic Society, 1971.

——. *The Zend Avesta of Zarathustra*. Cartago, Costa Rica: International Biogenic Society, 1973.

——. *Archeosophy, A New Science: Understanding Ancient Cultures*. Cartago, Costa Rica: International Biogenic Society, 1973.

——. *Pilgrim of the Himalayas: Life and Works of the Discoverer of Tibetan Buddhism*. Cartago, Costa Rica: International Biogenic Society, 1974.

——. *The Discovery of the Essene Gospel of Peace*. San Diego, CA: Academy Books, 1977.

Szlakmann, Charles. *Judaism for Beginners*. New York, NY: Writers and Readers Publishing, 1990.

Talbot, H. Fox. *The Antiquity of the Book of Genesis: Illustrated by Some New Arguments*. London, UK: Longman, Orme, Green, Brown, and Longman, 1839.

Talbot, Michael. *Mysticism and the New Physics*. New York, NY: Bantam, 1981.

Tannahill, Reay. *Sex in History*. 1980. Briarcliff Manor, NY: Scarborough, 1992 ed.

Tate, Karen. *Sacred Places of Goddess: 108 Destinations*. San Francisco, CA: Consortium of Collective Consciousness, 2006.

Tchakirides, Valjean. *The Shekhinah is Coming: Secrets of the Divine*. Bloomington, IN: Trafford, 2011.

Telushkin, Rabbi Joseph. *Jewish Literacy*. New York, NY: William Morrow and Co., 1991.

Temple, Theodore. *The Secret Discipline, Mentioned in Ancient Ecclesiastical History, Explained*. New York, NY: self-published (Samuel L. Knapp), 1833.

Tenney, Merrill C. (ed.). *Handy Dictionary of the Bible*. Grand Rapids, MI: Zondervan Publishing House, 1965.

Terapeut. *The Crucifixion, By an Eye-Witness: A Letter Written Seven Years After the Crucifixion, By a Personal Friend of Jesus in Jerusalem, to an Esseer [Essene] Brother in Alexandria*. 1907. Chicago, IL: Indo-American Book Co., 1911 ed.

Teresa, Saint (of Avila). *The Interior Castle, or the Mansions*. 1588. New York, NY: Benziger Brothers, 1912.

Testimonies of the Life, Character, Revelations and Doctrines of Mother Ann Lee, and the Elders With Her. Albany, NY: Shaker Heritage Society, 1888.

The Apocrypha: Translated Out of the Original Tongue. Cambridge, UK: Press Syndicate, n.d.

The Bhagavad Gita. Compiled from various writers. London, UK: The Christian Literature Society for India, 1899.

The Dhammapada: The Sayings of Buddha (6th Century B.C.). "Rendering" by Thomas Byrom. New York, NY: Vintage Books, 1976.

The Diamond Sutra and the Sutra of Hui Neng. Berkeley, CA: Shambala, 1973 ed.

The Epic of Gilgamesh (circa 3000 B.C.). N. K. Sandars, ed. 1960. Harmondsworth, England: Penguin, 1972 ed.

The Fortune Tellers. Baltimore: Black Watch, 1974.

The Fossil Record and Evolution: Collected articles from Scientific American. San Francisco, CA: W. H. Freeman and Co., 1982.

The Golden Manual: Or, Guide to Catholic Devotion, Public and Private. London, UK: Burns and Lambert, 1854.

The Illustrated World Encyclopedia. Woodbury, NY: Bobley Publishing Corp., 1977.

The Impersonal Life. 1941. San Gabriel, CA: C. A. Willing, 1973 ed.

The Koran (George Sale, trans.). 1734. London, UK: Frederick Warne and Co., n.d.

The Larousse Guide to Astronomy. David Baker. London, UK: Hamlyn Publishing, 1978.

The Layman's Parallel New Testament. 1970. Grand Rapids, MI.: Zondervan Publishing, 1977 ed.

The Literary Digest International Book Review, Vol. 4, No. 10, September 1926. New York: Funk and Wagnalls, 1926.

The New American Desk Encyclopedia. New York, NY: Signet, 1982.

The Secret Teachings of Jesus: Four Gnostic Gospels (Marvin W. Meyer, trans.). New York, NY: Random House, 1984.

The Story of the Bible. (Vol. 1: Genesis to Daniel.) New York, NY: Wm. H. Wise and Co., 1958.

The Thompson Chain-Reference Bible. King James Version. Indianapolis, IN: B. B. Kirkbride Bible Co., 1964.

The Times Atlas of World History. Maplewood, NJ: Hammond, 1989.

The Urantia Book: Revealing the Mysteries of God, the Universe, World History, Jesus, and Ourselves. 1955. Chicago, IL: Urantia Foundation, 2010 ed.

The World Almanac and Book of Facts. New York, NY: Pharos Books, 1990 ed.

The World Almanac and Book of Facts. New York, NY: Pharos Books, 1991 ed.

The World Book Encyclopedia. Chicago, IL: Field Enterprises Educational Corp., 1966 ed.

Thoreau, Henry David. *A Week on the Concord and Merrimack Rivers*. 1849. Boston, MA: James R. Osgood and Co., 1873 ed.

———. *Walden, or Life in the Woods*. 1854. Philadelphia, PA: Henry Artemus Co., 1899 ed.

Tichenor, Henry Mulford. *Tales of Theology: Jehovah, Satan and the Christian Creed*. St. Louis, MO: Melting Pot Publishing, 1918.

Tillich, Paul. *Dynamics of Faith*. New York, NY: Harper and Row, 1957.

Tingley, Katherine (ed.). *The Theosophical Path* (illustrated monthly). Vol. 16, January-July 1919. Point Loma, CA: New Century, 1919.

Titcomb, Sarah Elizabeth. *Aryan Sun-Myths: The Origin of Religions*. Troy, NY: Nims and Knight, 1889.

Tomlinson, Gerald. *Treasury of Religious Quotations*. Englewood Cliffs, NJ: Prentice Hall, 1991.

Tompkins, Peter. *Secrets of the Great Pyramid*. 1971. New York, NY: Harper Colophon Books, 1978 ed.

Torrey, Bradford (ed.). *The Writings of Henry David Thoreau: Journal, Vol. 1* (written 1837-1846). Boston, MA: Houghton, Mifflin and Co., 1906.

———. *The Writings of Henry David Thoreau: Journal, Vol. 3* (written 1851-1852). Boston, MA: Houghton, Mifflin and Co., 1906.

———. *The Writings of Henry David Thoreau: Journal, Vol. 9* (written 1856-1857). Boston, MA: Houghton, Mifflin and Co., 1906.

Torrey, Reuben Archer (ed.). *The Higher Criticism and the New Theology: Unscientific, Unscriptural, and Unwholesome*. New York: Gospel Publishing House, 1911.

Towns, Elmer L. *The Names of Jesus*. Denver, CO: Accent Publications, 1987.

Townsend, George Fyler. *"He Descended Into Hell": Observations on the Descent of Christ Into Hell*. London, UK: J. G. F. and J. Rivington, 1842.

Townsend, Mark. *Jesus Through Pagan Eyes: Bridging Neopagan Perspectives With a Progressive Vision of Christ*. Woodbury, MN: Llewellyn, 2012.

Toynbee, Arnold J. (trans.). *Greek Civilization and Character: The Self-Revelation of Ancient Greek Society*. New York, NY: Mentor, 1953.

Traupman, John C. *The New College Latin and English Dictionary*. 1966. New York, NY: Bantam, 1988 ed.

———. *The Bantam New College German and English Dictionary*. 1981. New York, NY: Bantam, 1986 ed.

Travis, Jerome. *Interspersed Harmony of the Life and Journeys of Christ*. Lansing, MI: Beacon Publishing Co., 1893.

Trench, Richard Chenevix. *Commentary on the Epistles to the Seven Churches in Asia*. New York, NY: Charles Scribner and Co., 1872.

Trine, Ralph Waldo. *In Tune With the Infinite; Or, Fullness of Peace, Power and Plenty*. 1897. New York, NY: Dodd, Mead and Co., 1921 ed.

Trollope, William. *Analecta Theologica: A Critical, Philological, and Exegetical Commentary on the New Testament*. 2 vols. London, UK: T. Cadell, 1830.

True Peace and Security: How Can You Find It? Brooklyn, NY: Watchtower Bible and Tract Society of New York, 1986.

Trunga, Chögyam. *Shambhala: The Sacred Path of the Warrior*. Boston, MA: Shambhala, 1988.

Tulloch, John. *The Christ of the Gospels and the Christ of Modern Criticism*. London, UK: Macmillan and Co., 1864.

Twain, Mark. *The Autobiography of Mark Twain*. 1917. New York, NY: Perennial Library, 1975 ed.

Ueberweg, Friedrich. *A History of Philosophy, From Thales to the Present Time*. 2 Vols. London: UK, 1872.

Underhill, Evelyn. *Mysticism: A Study of the Nature and Development of Man's Spiritual Consciousness*. 1911. New York, NY: E. P. Dutton and Co., 1961 ed.

———. *The Mystic Way: A Psychological Study in Christian Origins*. London, UK: J. M. Dent and Sons, 1914.

———. *Practical Mysticism: A Little Book for Normal People*. London, UK: J. M. Dent and Sons, 1914.

———. *The Essentials of Mysticism and Other Essays*. London, UK: J. M. Dent and Sons, 1920.

———. *The Life of the Spirit and the Life of Today*. New York, NY: E. P. Dutton and Co., 1922.

van Buitenen, J. A. B. (ed.). *The Bhagavadgita in the Mahabharata*. Chicago, IL: University of Chicago Press, 1981.

van der Toorn, Karel. *Scribal Culture and the Making of the Hebrew Bible*. Cambridge, MA: Harvard University Press, 2007.

Van Etten, Henry. *George Fox and the Quakers: Men of Wisdom* (E. Kelvin Osborn, trans.). London, UK: Longmans, 1959.

van Gelder, Dora. *The Real World of the Fairies*. Wheaton, IL: Quest, 1978.

Van Kolken, Diana. *Introducing the Shakers: An Explanation and Directory*. Bowling Green, OH: Gabriel's Horn Publishing, 1985.

van Loon, Hendrik Willem. *The Story of Mankind*. New York, NY: Boni and Liveright, 1921.

Van Voorst, Robert E. *Jesus Outside the New Testament: An Introduction to the Ancient Evidence*. Grand Rapids, MI: William B. Eerdmans, 2000.

Vaughan, James. *The Trident, the Crescent, and the Cross: A View of the Religious History of India During the Hindu, Buddhist, Mohammedan, and Christian Periods*. London, UK: Longmans, Green, and Co., 1876.

Venturini, Carl. *The Crucifixion by an Eye-Witness: A Letter, Written Seven Years After the Crucifixion, by a Personal Friend of Jesus in Jerusalem, to an Esseer [Essene] Brother in Alexandria*. Chicago-IL: Indo-American Book Co., 1915.

Vermes, Geza (ed.). *The Dead Sea Scrolls in English*. 1962. Harmondsworth, UK: Penguin, 1987 ed.

Versnel, H. S. *Coping With the Gods: Wayward Readings in Greek Theology*. Leiden, The Netherlands: Brill, 2011.

Vick, Robert L. *Contemporary Medical Physiology*. Menlo Park, CA: Addison-Wesley, 1984.

Volney, Constantin-François. *Volney's Ruins: Or Meditation on the Revolution of Empires* (Count Daru, trans.). New York, NY: G. Vale, 1853.

Von Däniken, Erich. *Chariots of the Gods? Unsolved Mysteries of the Past*. New York, NY: Bantam, 1968.

Wace, Henry, and Philip Schaff (eds.). *A Select Library of Nicene and Post-Nicene Fathers of the Christian Church*. Oxford, UK: James Parker and Co., 1894.

Wach, Joachim. *Sociology of Religion*. 1944. Chicago, IL: University of Chicago Press, 1971 ed.

Waggoner, Hyatt H. *American Poets: From the Puritans to the Present*. Boston, MA: Houghton Mifflin Co., 1968.

Wagiswara, W. D. C., and Kenneth James Saunders. *The Buddha's "Way of Virtue": A Translation of the Dhammapada from the Pali Text*. London, UK: John Murray, 1912.

Wahr, Frederick B. *Emerson and Goethe: Emerson and the Germans*. Ann Arbor, MI: George Wahr, 1915.

Waite, Arthur Edward. *A Book of Mystery and Vision*. London, UK: Philip Wellby, 1902.

Walker, Barbara G. *The Women's Encyclopedia of Myths and Secrets*. San Francisco, CA: Harper and Row, 1983.

——. *The Crone: Woman of Age, Wisdom, and Power*. New York, NY: Harper and Row, 1985.

——. *The Women's Dictionary of Symbols and Sacred Objects*. San Francisco, CA: Harper and Row, 1988.

Walker, Edward Dwight. *Reincarnation: A Study of Forgotten Truth*. New York, NY: John W. Lovell, 1888.

Wall, Otto Augustus. *Sex and Sex Worship*. St. Louis, MO: C. V. Mosby Co., 1919.

Wallace, Anthony F. C. *Religion: An Anthropological View*. New York, NY: Random House, 1966.

Walton, Robert C. *Chronological and Background Charts of Church History*. Grand Rapids, MI: Academie Books, 1986.

Walvoord, John F. *The Rapture Question: A Comprehensive Biblical Study of the Translation of the Church*. 1957. Grand Rapids, MI: Zondervan, 1970 ed.

Ward, C. H. S. *The Ethics of Gotama Buddha: An Appreciation and a Criticism*. Kandy, Sri Lanka: self-published, 1923.

Ward, John. *Zion's Works: New Light on the Bible*. 16 vols. London, UK: John MacQueen, 1899-1904.

Warnock, Robert, and George K. Anderson. *The Ancient Foundations*. 1950. Glenview, IL: Scott, Foresman and Co., 1967 ed.

Watts, Alan W. *The Supreme Identity*. 1950. New York, NY: Vintage, 1972 ed.

——. *Behold the Spirit (A Study in the Necessity of Mystical Religion)*. 1947. New York, NY: Vintage, 1972 ed.

——. *The Wisdom of Insecurity*. New York, NY: Vintage, 1951.

——. *The Way of Zen*. 1957. New York, NY: Mentor, 1960 ed.

——. *The Joyous Cosmology: Adventures in the Chemistry of Consciousness*. New York, NY: Vintage, 1962.

——. *The Book On the Taboo Against Knowing Who You Are*. 1966. New York, NY: Collier, 1971 ed.

——. *Does it Matter? Essays on Man's Relation to Materiality*. 1968. New York, NY: Vintage, 1971 ed.

——. *Myth and Ritual in Christianity*. Boston, MA: Beacon Press, 1968.

——. *Cloud-Hidden, Whereabouts Unknown*. 1968. New York, NY: Vintage, 1974 ed.

——. *This Is It and Other Essays On Zen and Spiritual Experience*. 1958. New York, NY: Collier, 1970 ed.

——. *In My Own Way: An Autobiography*. 1972. New York, NY: Vintage, 1973 ed.

——. *God* (Book 1 of the series, "The Essence of Alan Watts"). Millbrae, CA: Celestial Arts, 1974.

Webster's Biographical Dictionary. Springfield, MA: G. and C. Merriam Co., 1943.

Weems, Mason Locke. *The Life of Benjamin Franklin; With Many Choice Anecdotes and Admirable Sayings of This Great Man, Never Before Published By Any of His Biographers*. Philadelphia, PA: Uriah Hunt's Sons, 1873.

Weigall, Arthur Edward Pearse Brome. *The Paganism In Our Christianity*. London, UK: Hutchinson and Co., 1928.

Weigel, James, Jr. *Mythology*. Lincoln, NE: Cliff Notes, 1973.

Wells, G. A. *The Historical Evidence for Jesus*. Buffalo, NY: Prometheus Books, 1988.

Wells, H. G. *The Outline of History*. 2 Vols. 1920. Garden City, NY: Garden City Books, 1961 ed.

Wessels, Cornelius. *Early Jesuit Travellers in Central Asia: 1603-1721*. The Hague, Netherlands:

Martinus Nijhoff, 1924.

Westbrook, Richard Brodhead. *The Eliminator; or, Skeleton Keys to Sacerdotal Secrets*. Philadelphia, PA: J. B. Lippincott, 1894.

Westcott, Frank N. *Catholic Principles*. Milwaukee, WI: The Young Churchman Co., 1902.

Westcott, W. Wynn. *The Occult Power of Numbers*. North Hollywood, CA: Newcastle Publishing, 1984.

Whale, J. S. *Christian Doctrine*. 1941. London, UK: Collins, 1960 ed.

Wheeler, Joseph Mazzini. *Frauds and Follies of the Early Church Fathers: With a Review of The Worth of Their Testimony to the Four Gospels*. London, UK: Freethought Publishing Co., 1882.

White, Anne Terry. *The Golden Treasury of Myths and Legends*. New York, NY: Golden Press, 1959.

White, Ellen G. *The Desire of Ages: The Conflict of the Ages Illustrated in the Life of Christ*. 1898. Mountain View, CA: Pacific Press, 1940 ed.

White, Jon E. Manchip. *Everyday Life in Ancient Egypt*. New York, NY: Perigee, 1963.

———. *Ancient Egypt: Its Culture and History*. New York, NY: Dover, 1970.

Whitehead, Alfred North. *Religion in the Making*. 1926. New York, NY: Mentor, 1974 ed.

Whitehouse, Ruth, and John Wilkins. *The Making of Civilization*. London, UK: Roxby Archaeology, 1986.

Whitman, Walt. *Leaves of Grass*. 1855-1892. Philadelphia, PA: Rees Welsh and Co., 1882 ed.

Whitney, Loren Harper. *Life and Teachings of Zoroaster, the Great Persian: Including a Comparison of the Persian and Hebrew Religions Showing That "The Word of the Lord" Came to the Hebrews by Way of Persia, and Offering Proof That the Jews Copied Heavily From the Hindu Bible*. Chicago, IL: self-published, 1905.

———. *A Question of Miracles: Parallels in the Lives of Buddha and Jesus*. Chicago, IL: The Library Shelf, 1908.

Wickens, Rev. Paul A. *Christ Denied: Origin of the Present Day Problems in the Catholic Church*. Rockford, IL: Tan Books, 1982.

Wiener, Leo (ed. and trans.). *The Complete Works of Count Tolstoy, Vol. 14: The Four Gospels Harmonized and Translated, by Tolstoy*. Boston, MA: Dana Estes and Co., 1904.

Wight, Fred H. *Manners and Customs of Bible Lands*. Chicago, IL: Moody Press, 1953.

Wilbur, Sibyl. *The Life of Mary Baker Eddy*. 1907. Boston, MA: Christian Science Publishing, 1976 ed.

Wilhelm, Anthony J. *Christ Among Us: A Modern Presentation of the Catholic Faith*. New York, NY: Newman Press, 1967.

Wilkinson, John Gardner. *The Egyptians in the Time of the Pharoahs*. London, UK: Bradbury and Evans, 1857.

William Shakespeare: The Complete Works. New York, NY: Dorset Press, 1988.

Williams, Howard (trans.). *Lucian's Dialogues*. London, UK: George Bell and Sons, 1888.

Williams, Watkin. *St. Bernard: The Man and His Message*. Manchester, UK: Manchester University Press, 1944.

Wilson, Bryan R. *Religion in a Secular Society*. 1966. Harmondsworth, UK: Penguin, 1969 ed.

Wilson, Colin. *The Occult: A History*. New York, NY: Random House, 1972.

Wilson, Edward O. *Sociobiology: The New Synthesis*. Cambridge, MA: Belknap Press, 1975.

———. *On Human Nature*. New York, NY: Bantam New Age, 1979.

Wilson, John Rowan. *The Mind*. 1964. New York, NY: Time-Life Books, 1968 ed.

Winder, Delores, and Bill Keith. *Jesus Set Me Free*. Safety Harbor, FL: Fellowship Foundation, 1983.

Windle, Charles Augustus. *Christian vs. Pagan Civilization: Truth About the Catholic Church*. Chicago, IL: Iconoclast Publishing Co., 1914.

Wingeier, Douglas E. *Paul: His Life*. Nashville, TN: Graded Press, 1987.

Winick, Charles. *Dictionary of Anthropology*. Totowa, NJ: Littlefield, Adams and Co., 1970.

Winternitz, Moriz. *A General Index to the Names and Subject-matter of The Sacred Books of the East*. Oxford, UK: Clarendon Press, 1910.

———. *A Concise Dictionary of Eastern Religion*. Oxford, UK: Clarendon Press, 1910.

Wise, Micahel, Martin Abegg Jr., and Edward Cook. *The Dead Sea Scrolls: A New Translation*. San Francisco, CA: Harper Collins, 1996.

Wong, Kiew Kit. *Sukhavati, Western Paradise: Going to Heaven as Taught by the Buddha*. Sungai Petani,

Kedah, Malaysia: Cosmos Internet Sdn Bhd, 2002.
Wood, James. *A Dictionary of the Holy Bible*. 2 vols. New York, NY: Griffin and Rudd, 1813.
Woolger, Jennifer Barker, and Roger J. Woolger. *The Goddess Within: A Guide to the Eternal Myths That Shape Women's Lives*. New York, NY: Fawcett Columbine, 1989.
Wordsworth, Christopher. *The New Testament of Our Lord and Saviour Jesus Christ, In the Original Greek*. London, UK: Rivingtons, 1861.
———. *The Holy Bible, In the Authorized Version*. 12 vols. London, UK: Rivingtons, 1873.
Wouk, Herman. *This Is My God*. 1959. New York, NY: Touchstone, 1986 ed.
Wright, Conrad (ed.). *Three Prophets of Religious Liberalism: Channing, Emerson, Parker*. 1961. Boston, MA: Unitarian Universalist Association, 1980 ed.
Wright, G. Frederick, William G. Ballantine, and Frank H. Foster (eds.). *The Bibliotheca Sacra*. Vol. 48. Oberlin, OH: E. J. Goodrich, 1891.
Yamada, Keichyu. *Scenes From the Life of Buddha*. Chicago, IL: Open Court, 1898.
Yoder, John H. *The Original Revolution: Essays on Christian Pacifism*. 1971. Scottsdale, PA: Herald Press, 1977 ed.
———. *The Politics of Jesus*. 1972. Grand Rapids, MI: William B. Eerdmans Publishing Co., 1983 ed.
Yogananda, Paramahansa. *Autobiography of a Yogi*. 1946. Los Angeles, CA: Self-Realization Fellowship, 1972 ed.
———. *Whispers From Eternity*. Los Angeles, CA: Self-Realization Fellowship, 1973.
———. *The Second Coming of Christ: The Resurrection of the Christ Within You*. 2 vols. Los Angeles, CA: Self-Realization Fellowship, 2004.
You Can Live Forever In Paradise on Earth. Brooklyn, NY: Watchtower Bible and Tract Society of New York, 1982, 1989.
Young, Dudley. *Origins of the Sacred: The Ecstacies of Love and War*. 1991. New York, NY: Harper Perennial, 1992 ed.
Young, G. Douglas (ed.). *Young's Compact Bible Dictionary*. 1984. Wheaton, IL: Tyndale House, 1989 ed.
Zaehner, R. C. (ed.). *Encyclopedia of the World's Religions*. 1959. New York, NY: Barnes and Noble, 1997 ed.
Zarandi, Nabil. *The Dawn-Breakers: Nabil's Narrative of the Early Days of the Baha'i Revelation*. Evanston, IL: Bahai Publishing Trust, 1974, reprint.
Ziegenbalg, Bartholomaeus. *Genealogy of the South-Indian Gods: A Manual of the Mythology and Religion of the People of Southern India, Including a Popular Description of Hinduism*. Madras, India: Higginbotham and Co., 1869.
Zimmerman, J. E. *Dictionary of Classical Mythology*. New York, NY: Bantam, 1964.
Zinner, Samuel. *The Gospel of Thomas: In the Light of Early Jewish, Christian and Islamic Esoteric Trajectories*. London, UK: Matheson Trust, 2011.
Ziolkowski, Eric (ed.). *The Bible in Folklore Worldwide: A Handbook of Biblical Reception in Folklores of Africa, Asia, Oceania, and the Americas*. Berlin, Germany: Walter de Gruyter, 2023.
Zolar. *Zolar's Encyclopedia of Ancient and Forbidden Knowledge*. 1970. New York, NY: Fireside, 1984 ed.
Zöllner, Johann Carl Friedrich. *Transcendental Physics: An Account of Experimental Investigations From the Scientific Treatises*. London, UK: W. H. Harrison, 1880.
Zondervan Compact Bible Dictionary. 1967. Grand Rapids, MI: Zondervan Publishing House, 1993 ed.

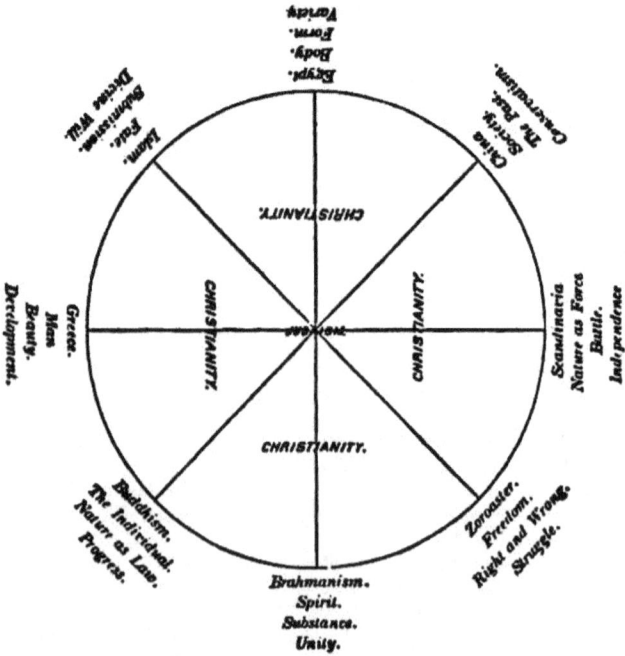

An 1871 diagram by comparative religionist James Freeman Clarke, showing how he believed the world's ten great religions are related.

Index

INCLUDES TOPICS, PEOPLE, KEYWORDS, KEY PHRASES, & SPELLING VARIATIONS

MEET THE AUTHOR

NEO-VICTORIAN SCHOLAR LOCHLAINN SEABROOK, a descendant of the families of Alexander Hamilton Stephens, John Singleton Mosby, Edmund Winchester Rucker, and William Giles Harding, is a 7th generation Kentuckian and one of the most prolific and widely read writers in the world today. Known by literary critics as the "new Shelby Foote," the "American Robert Graves," and the "Southern Joseph Campbell," and by his fans as the "Voice of the Traditional South," he is a recipient of the United Daughters of the Confederacy's prestigious Jefferson Davis Historical Gold Medal, and is considered the foremost Southern interpreter of American Civil War history—or what he refers to as the War for the Constitution (1861-1865). A lifelong nonfiction writer, the Sons of Confederate Veterans member has authored and edited books ranging in topics from history, politics, science, comparative religion, spirituality, astronomy, entertainment, military, biography, and Bible studies, to nature, music, humor, gastronomy, etymology, onomastics, mysteries, alternative health, comparative mythology, genealogy, and the paranormal; books that his readers describe as "game changers," "transformative," and "life altering."

One of the world's most popular living historians, he is a 17th generation Southerner of Appalachian heritage who descends from dozens of patriotic Revolutionary War soldiers and Confederate soldiers from Kentucky, Tennessee, North Carolina, and Virginia. Also a history, wildlife, and nature preservationist, the well-respected polymath began life as a child prodigy, later maturing into an archetypal Renaissance Man. Besides being an accomplished and esteemed author, historian, biographer, creative, and Bible authority, the influential litterateur is also a Kentucky Colonel, eagle scout, entrepreneur, screenwriter, nature, wildlife, and landscape photographer and videographer, artist, graphic designer, content creator, genealogist, former history museum docent, and a former ranch hand, zookeeper, and wrangler. A songwriter (of some 3,000 songs in a dozen genres), he is also a film composer, multi-instrument musician, vocalist, session player, and music producer who has worked and performed with some of Nashville's top musicians and singers.

Currently Seabrook is the multi-genre author and editor of nearly 100 adult and children's books (totaling some 30,000 pages and 15,000,000 words) that have earned him accolades from around the globe. His works, which have sold on every continent except Antarctica, have introduced hundreds of thousands to vital facts that have been left out of our mainstream books. He has been endorsed internationally by leading experts, museum curators, award-winning historians, bestselling authors, celebrities, filmmakers, noted scientists, well regarded educators, TV show hosts and producers, renowned military artists, venerable heritage organizations, and distinguished academicians of all races, creeds, and colors.

Of northern, western, and central European ancestry, he is the 6th great-grandson of the Earl of Oxford and a descendant of European royalty through his Kentucky father and West Virginia mother. His modern day cousins include: Johnny Cash, Elvis Presley, Lisa Marie Presley, Billy Ray and Miley Cyrus, Patty Loveless, Tim McGraw, Lee Ann Womack, Dolly Parton, Pat Boone, Naomi, Wynonna, and Ashley Judd, Ricky Skaggs, the Sunshine Sisters, Martha Carson, Chet Atkins, Patrick J. Buchanan, Cindy Crawford, Bertram Thomas Combs ntucky's 50th governor), Edith Bolling (second wife of President Woodrow Wilson), Andy Griffith, Riley Keough, George C. Scott, Robert Duvall, Reese Witherspoon, Lee Marvin, Rebecca Gayheart, and Tom Cruise.

A constitutionalist, avid outdoorsman, and gun rights advocate, Seabrook is the author of the international blockbuster, *Everything You Were Taught About the Civil War is Wrong, Ask a Southerner!* He lives with his wife and family in the magnificent Rocky Mountains, heart of the American West, where you will find him hiking, filming, and writing.

For more information on author Mr. Seabrook visit

LOCHLAINNSEABROOK.COM

Keep Your Body, Mind, & Spirit Vibrating at Their Highest Level!

YOU CAN DO SO BY READING THE BOOKS OF

SEA RAVEN PRESS

There is nothing that will so perfectly keep your body, mind, and spirit in a healthy condition as to think wisely and positively. Hence you should not only read this book, but also the other books that we offer. They will quicken your physical, mental, and spiritual vibrations, enabling you to maintain a position in society as a healthy erudite person.

KEEP YOURSELF WELL-INFORMED!

The well-informed person is always at the head of the procession, while the ignorant, the lazy, and the unthoughtful hang onto the rear. If you are a Spiritual man or woman, do yourself a great favor: read Sea Raven Press books and stay well posted on the Truth. It is almost criminal for one to remain in ignorance while the opportunity to gain knowledge is open to all at a nominal price.

We invite you to visit our Webstore for a wide selection of wholesome, family-friendly, well-researched, educational books for all ages. You will be glad you did!

Artisan-Crafted Books & Merch From the Rocky Mountains!

SeaRavenPress.com

LochlainnSeabrook.com
TheBestCivilWarBookEver.com
AmbianceGoneWild.com
Shutterstock.com/g/Lochlainn+Seabrook
Pond5.com/artist/LochlainnSeabrook

If you enjoyed this book, you will be interested in Mr. Seabrook's other popular related titles:

☞ SEABROOK'S BIBLE DICTIONARY OF TRADITIONAL AND MYSTICAL CHRISTIAN DOCTRINES
☞ JESUS & THE LAW OF ATTRACTION: THE BIBLE-BASED GUIDE TO CREATING PERFECT HEALTH, WEALTH, AND HAPPINESS FOLLOWING CHRIST'S SIMPLE FORMULA
☞ JESUS & THE GOSPEL OF Q: CHRIST'S PRE-CHRISTIAN TEACHINGS AS RECORDED IN THE NEW TESTAMENT
☞ CHRIST IS ALL & IN ALL: REDISCOVERING YOUR DIVINE NATURE & THE KINGDOM WITHIN
☞ CHRISTMAS BEFORE CHRISTIANITY: HOW THE BIRTHDAY OF THE "SUN" BECAME THE BIRTHDAY OF THE "SON"
☞ BRITANNIA RULES: GODDESS-WORSHIP IN ANCIENT ANGLO-CELTIC SOCIETY

Available from Sea Raven Press and wherever fine books are sold

ALL OF OUR BOOK COVERS ARE AVAILABLE AS 11" X 17" POSTERS, SUITABLE FOR FRAMING.

SEARAVENPRESS.COM